ENGLISH
FOR ADULT
COMPETENCY
BOOK ONE

ENGLISH FOR ADULT COMPETENCY

BOOK ONE

SAN DIEGO
COMMUNITY COLLEGE DISTRICT

Autumn Keltner, Leann Howard, Frances Lee
with
Virginia Kellner, Anne Walker, Jeanine Eberhardt, Caroline Hamlin

Illustrations by Mark Neyndorff

Prentice-Hall, Inc., Englewood Cliffs, New Jersey 07632

Library of Congress Cataloging in Publication Data

KELTNER, AUTUMN.
  English for adult competency.

   Vol. 2 by A. Keltner and G. Bitterlin.
   1. English Language—Text-books for foreigners.
I. Howard, Leann, joint author. II. Lee, Frances,
1927– joint author. III. Bitterlin, Gretchen,
joint author. IV. San Diego Community College
District. V. Title.
PE1128.K423 1981   428.2′4   80-16851
ISBN 0-13-279745-3 (v. 1)

Printed in the United States of America

10 9 8 7 6 5 4 3 2 1

Editorial/production supervision by Diane Lange
Interior design by Emily Dobson
Cover design by 20/20 Services, Inc.
Manufacturing buyer: Harry P. Baisley

PRENTICE-HALL INTERNATIONAL, INC., *London*
PRENTICE-HALL OF AUSTRALIA PTY. LIMITED, *Sydney*
PRENTICE-HALL OF CANADA, LTD., *Toronto*
PRENTICE-HALL OF INDIA PRIVATE LIMITED, *New Delhi*
PRENTICE-HALL OF JAPAN, INC., *Tokyo*
PRENTICE-HALL OF SOUTHEAST ASIA PTE. LTD., *Singapore*
WHITEHALL BOOKS LIMITED, WELLINGTON, *New Zealand*

Contents

6 Clothing and Fabrics

7 Looking for a Job

8 Banking and Postal Services

9 Community Resources

Foreword

English for Adult Competency, Books 1 and 2 are a basic guide for teachers whose adult students need to learn the oral language patterns and vocabulary required in real-life situations. They provide classroom teachers with effective materials that are relevant to the immediate needs of limited- or non-English speaking adults.

Book 1 is aimed primarily at developing the listening and speaking skills of adults who have had little or no previous instruction in English, so that they may communicate effectively in the following content areas:

I.	Identification and Communication
II.	Food and Money
III.	Health Care
IV.	Transportation
V.	Housing
VI.	Clothing and Fabrics
VII.	Looking for a Job
VIII.	Banking and Postal Services
IX.	Community Resources

The units are situation-oriented, non-sequential, and minimally structured. They should not be considered solely as grammar lessons. Their primary purpose is to develop immediately useable oral communication skills. The material takes the students beyond the level of merely knowing *about* the new language, beyond the ability to repeat memorized dialogues and beyond mechanical substitutions of one word or structure item for another.

Both books contain competency objectives, structure focus, pre-post assessments, dialogues, structure and vocabulary practice, visuals and supplemental activities. Book 1 also has reading exercises.

The competency objectives, stated in performance terms, indicate functional competencies that the student will have achieved upon the successful completion of each unit. They are keyed to the goals and objectives of the Adult Performance Level (APL—University of Texas at Austin) project as revised by the American College Testing Program.

It is the task of the teacher to determine which units are most needed and to provide sufficient practice, reinforcement, and opportunities for the students to communicate meaningfully (become competent) in the situations which they will encounter in their daily lives.

Teaching Guidelines

It is strongly recommended that the teacher read through and study each unit carefully before presenting it to the class. The teacher will then have a clear idea of the unit objectives, how to integrate the visuals, and where to incorporate the supplemental activities.

Pre-Post Assessments   The pre-post assessments determine the level of mastery before and after each unit has been presented. In Book 1 many of the assessment tasks are keyed to visuals. Most of the student responses will be oral because the reading and writing skills of beginning ESL students are usually limited. The assessment may be done on an individual basis if time and staffing permit. Otherwise the activity may be given to the group as a whole or to small groups or pairs of students. The teacher circulates to determine the correctness of the responses. If competency is demonstrated in certain areas, those topics need not be covered.

Dialogues   The dialogues represent simulated real-life situations in which the students communicate a need or response. The dialogues introduce these situations through structures containing the basic elements of the language.

The dialogues are modeled by the teacher (books are closed). Students should hear the complete dialogue two or three times. The teacher presents the situation using pictures, gestures, pantomime, or whatever is necessary to get the meaning across. If an aide is available, teacher and aide may each take a part.

After this demonstration the students repeat each section after the teacher. Next the teacher divides the class in half. One half assumes one role, the second half, the other. The roles can then be reversed. Finally, individual students may act out the dialogue. Only now should the students open their books to read the dialogue.

Practices   A series of practice exercises usually follows each dialogue. They are directly related to the context of the dialogue and serve as reinforcement for the basic vocabulary, structure, and context for each unit.

Two basic types of practices are used. The *repetition* practice focuses the student's attention on the pattern to be learned and is usually short enough to be repeated easily. The teacher signals for the students to listen and models the pattern several times with normal intonation and at normal speed. The teacher then signals for the whole group (half groups, rows, individuals) to repeat several times.

The substitution practices provide additional reinforcement of the structure or vocabulary presented in the repetitions. Students focus on substituting one word in the model sentence (noun replaced by another noun, verb by another verb, adjective by another adjective). At first a substitution drill is cued with spoken words. Later, concrete objects, pictures, or written words may be used to cue the substitution.

Example:	Teacher:	What's your zip code?	
	Students:	What's your zip code?	
	Teacher:	What's your zip code?	(his)
	Students:	What's his zip code?	
	Teacher:	What's his zip code?	(her)
	Students:	What's her zip code?	
	Teacher:	What's her zip code?	

It is extremely important and necessary for the teacher to *repeat* the correct response after the students have said it. This provides the positive reinforcement needed for mastery.

Reading Exercises   These exercises review the information presented in each unit and assess reading comprehension. In these individual activities the students read and answer questions either orally or in writing. The teacher then asks the last group of questions which are related to the students' own lives. Students may be paired to elicit the information from each other. If some students are unable to read, the teacher or aide can work with them individually or as a group while the rest of the class works independently.

Using the Visuals   An integral part of each unit is formed by the visuals used with each dialogue and the "whole page visuals". These adult-oriented visuals add realism and relevance when used in 1) setting the scene for the situations in the dialogues, 2) developing the topics for each unit, 3) relating the activities to adult students' own experiences, and 4) evaluating student mastery of structure, content, vocabulary, and concepts. Suggested activities for using each visual are provided.

Supplemental Activities Suggested supplemental activities for providing additional practice and reinforcement of the vocabulary and concepts are included in each unit. These activities include games, paired activities, questions and responses, and role-playing. In many instances role-playing has been suggested as an activity or an evaluative tool. In this activity the teacher assigns roles to individual students, who then act out a designated situation. In a role-play the student can play himself in a simulated situation or take a fictitious part. Students usually feel more free to express themselves when they are being someone else. Role-play differs from simply acting out a dialogue, as it requires students to improvise using vocabulary, structures, concepts, and cultural information previously presented and practiced.

The teacher sets the scene for the role-playing by explaining the situation and describing the task to be accomplished. After useful vocabulary and expressions and general background information have been discussed, roles are assigned. Students are then given time to practice before the improvisation is presented. When using role-play as an evaluative tool the teacher should only describe the task and assign the roles.

The primary goal of role-playing is to provide an opportunity for students to use English for real communication.

1

Identification and Communication

COMPETENCY OBJECTIVES

On completion of this unit the students will show orally, in writing, or through demonstration that they are able to use the language needed to function in the following situations.

A. PERSONAL INFORMATION AND INTRODUCTIONS
1. Give, upon request, self-identification and personal information, including: name, address, telephone number, place of birth, age, Social Security number, nationality, education, marital status, and occupation.

2. Fill out simple forms.

3. Give and respond to simple greetings.

4. Make and respond to simple introductions.

B. STATES OF BEING/FEELINGS
Express feelings and states of being.

C. FAMILY RELATIONSHIPS
Identify members of immediate and extended family.

D. TELLING TIME
1. Tell time in minutes and hours.

2. Identify periods of time in days, months, and years.

E. TELEPHONE COMMUNICATION
1. Dial given numbers.

2. Answer incoming calls.

3. Take simple messages.

Pre-Post Assessment

A. PERSONAL INFORMATION AND INTRODUCTIONS

Evaluation is made by assessing the students' competence in both asking and responding to questions. This procedure can be accomplished by (a) having students work in pairs, with teacher and aide (if available) circulating and assessing, or (b) having teacher and/or aide make individual assessments.

1. Looking at the Personal Information visual, have the students answer these questions:

   a. What's your name?
   b. What's your address?
   c. What's your zip code?
   d. What's your telephone number?
   e. What's your Social Security number?
   f. What's your name?
   g. Where are you from?
   h. What's your date of birth?
   i. When were you born?
   j. Are you married?
   k. Are you single?
   l. What's your occupation?

2. Using the forms on page 8 , have the students fill in the blanks.

3. Have the students role-play the following situations, in which two students meet:

   a. They exchange greetings.
   b. One student from each pair introduces his/her friend to the others.

B. STATES OF BEING/FEELINGS

Have the students look at the States of Being/Feelings visual, and tell about each picture. (*Example:* She is busy. I am hungry.)

C. FAMILY RELATIONSHIPS

Using the Family visual, have the students name the members of the family. (*Example:* She is the mother. He is the grandfather.)

D. TELLING TIME

1. Using a cardboard or plastic clock, have the students tell time in hour, half-hour, minutes.

2. Using a large calendar or transparency, have the students tell the day, month, and year.

E. TELEPHONE COMMUNICATION

Using plastic telephones or the tele-trainer from the telephone company, have the students role-play the following situations:

1. Dial a given number.

2. One caller gives a simple message; the other student takes the message.

How Are You?

A. Hello. How are you?
B. Fine, thank you. And you?
A. Just fine, thanks.

PRACTICE

Hello. How are you?
Good morning.
Good afternoon.
Good evening.

Fine, thank you.
Just fine,
Very well,

I'm Happy To Meet You.

A. Bill, this is Tom.
B. I'm happy to meet you, Tom.
A. Thank you. The same to you.

PRACTICE

Bill, this is Tom.
    my wife.
    my husband.
    my teacher.

I'm happy to meet you.
glad
pleased

What's Your Name?

A. Hello. This is your school registration card. What's your name?

B. My name is Joe Brown.

A. What's your address?

B. My address is 1632 Broadway Street.

A. What's your zip code?

B. It's 92102.

PRACTICE

What's your name?
         first name?
         last name?
         family name?
         middle name?

What's your address?
         telephone number?
         Social Security number?

What's your zip code?
      their
      his/her

1 — one	6 — six
2 — two	7 — seven
3 — three	8 — eight
4 — four	9 — nine
5 — five	10 — ten

Miss Helen Park
734 Oak Street
Austin, Texas 78768

Mr. Joe Brown
1130 Olympia Way
San Francisco, CA
           94131

Mrs. Mary King
195 Congress Street
Brooklyn, NY
        11201

Mr. and Mrs. T. J. Lim
613 West Avenue
Los Angeles, CA
          11365

Where Are You From?

A. I'm from Japan.
   Where are you from?
B. I'm from Mexico.
A. Is your wife from Mexico, too?
B. No, she's from Cuba.

PRACTICE

I am   from Mexico.
You are
He/She/It is

I'm from Japan.
You're   Mexico.
He's   California.
She's   Florida.
They're Iran.

You are   from Mexico.
He/She/it is
You are
We are
They are

Is your wife from Mexico, too?
       husband
       teacher

Where were you born?
Where are you from?
What is your birthplace?

We are   from Mexico.
You are
They are

Are you   from Mexico?
Is he/she/it
Are we
Are you
Are they

Your Job

A. What is your occupation?
B. What?
A. What is your job?
B. What?
A. What do you *do*?
B. Oh, I go to school. I'm a student.

PRACTICE

What is your occupation?
           job?
           work?

I'm a student.
     housewife.
     mechanic.

I go to school.   We go to school.
You go   You go
He/She/It goes   They go

What kind of job do you have?
           work   do?

I'm unemployed.
     retired.
     out of work.

1

2

3

4

5

6

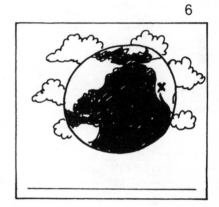

7

8

9

Name
Mr.
Mrs.
Ms. _____   Sex: M ☐
F ☐

Last   First   Middle

Address _____

Number   Street

_____

City   State   Zip Code   Telephone

Name
Mr.
Mrs.
Ms. _____   Sex: M ☐
F ☐

Last   First   Middle

Address _____

Number   Street

_____

City   State   Zip Code   Telephone

_____

Date of Birth   Place of Birth

Name
Mr.
Mrs.
Ms. _____   Male ☐
Female ☐

Address _____

Number   Street

City   State   Zip Code   Social Security No.

Telephone   Date of Birth   Place of Birth

How Do You Feel?

A. How do you feel?
B. Tired! How about you?
A. No, I'm not tired, but I'm sleepy.

PRACTICE

How do you feel?
    does she
    does he

I'm tired. How about you?
    sleepy.
    hungry.
    thirsty.
    busy.
    happy.

I am tired.
You are tired.
He/she is tired.

We are tired.
You are tired.
They are tired.

You are hungry.
He is
She is
They are

I am *not* tired.
You are *not* tired.
He/She is *not* tired.

We are *not* tired.
You are *not* tired.
They are *not* tired.

Are you hungry?
Is he
Is she
Are they

1

2

3

4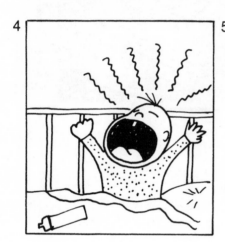

5

6

7

8

9

Your Family

A. Are you married?

B. Yes, I am.

A. Tell me about your family.
How many children do you have?

B. I have two children, one son,
and one daughter.

PRACTICE

Tell me about your family.
               husband.
               wife.
               children.

one child — two children
one man — two men
one woman — two women

How many children do you have?
               does he/she have?

I have two children.   We have two children.
You have   You have
He/She has   They have

Are You Married?

A. Are you married?
B. No, I'm not. I'm single.
A. Do you live with your parents?
B. No, I don't. They live in New York.

PRACTICE

Do you live with your parents?
                grandparents?
                aunt?
                uncle?
                cousins?

Do you live with your parents?
         near

I live in New York.	I don't live in New York.
You live	You don't
He/She *lives*	He/She doesn't *live*
We live in New York.	We don't live in New York.
You live	You don't
They live	They don't

do not — don't
does not — doesn't

How Old Are Your Children?

A. How old are your children?

B. My son is 16 years old.
   My daughter is 10.

A. Are they in school?

B. Yes. He's a junior in high school.
   She's in elementary school.

PRACTICE

How old are your children?
                  his
                  her
                  their

She's in preschool.
        elementary school.
        junior high school.
        senior high school.
        college.

How old are you?
What is your age?
What is your date of birth?
When is your birthday?
When were you born?

What's The Date?

A. What day is it?
B. It's Wednesday.
A. What's the date?
B. It's April 14, 19___.
A. Is it the fourteenth?
B. Yes, I'm sure it is.

PRACTICE

It's Monday.
    Tuesday.
    Wednesday.
    Thursday.
    Friday.
    Saturday.
    Sunday.

It's January.
    February.
    March.
    April.
    May.
    June.
    July.
    August.
    September.
    October.
    November.
    December.

It's the first.
    second.
    third.
    fourth.
    fifth.
    sixth.
    seventh.
    eighth.
    ninth.
    tenth.
    eleventh.
    twelfth.
    thirteenth.
    twentieth.

When's the picnic?
    Christmas?
    Easter?
    your birthday?

Hello, It's For You

A. Hello.

B. Hello. This is Bill. Is Tom there?

A. Yes. Just a minute, please.
Tom, it's for you.

PRACTICE

Just a minute, please.
    moment
    second

Tom, it's for you.
    me.
    him.
    her.
    us.
    them.

Is Sue There?

A. Hello.

B. Hello. Is Sue there?

A. No, she's not. May I take a message?

B. Yes. This is Tom. Please tell her
I'll call later.

A. All right, I will. Goodbye.

PRACTICE

Tell her I'll call later.
    tomorrow.
    next week.
    back.

I'll call her next week.
You'll
He'll
She'll
They'll

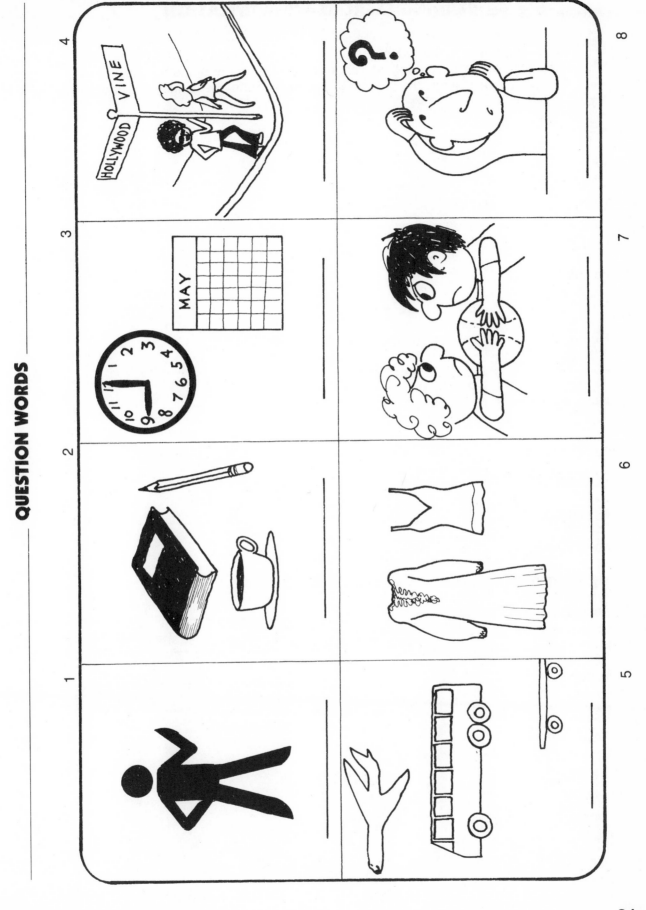

His name is Jose. He comes to school to study English. He is from Mexico. He is a student. At school he meets many students. He is not married. He is single; he lives with his cousin. Today he is busy and happy.

Questions

1. What is his name?
2. Where is he from?
3. What does he study?
4. How does he feel today?

Write the Word

1. His _____ is Jose.

2. He comes _____ school to study English.

3. He _____ a student.

4. He is not married; he is _____.

Write About You

1. My name is _____.

2. I am from _____.

3. My address is _____.

4. My zip code is _____.

5. I come to school to study _____.

6. I am a _____.

7. Today I feel _____.

Using The Visuals

A. PERSONAL INFORMATION

1. Pair the students. Have students ask and respond to these questions, giving personal information about themselves.

   a. What's your name?
   b. What's your address?/Where do you live?
   c. What's your zip code?
   d. What's your telephone number/area code?
   e. What's your Social Security number?
   f. Where are you from?
   g. What's your birthdate?
   h. Are you married? Are you single?
   i. What's your occupation/job?

B. STATES OF BEING/FEELINGS

With students looking at the visual or using an overhead transparency:

1. Have the students tell about the pictures.

   a. She's busy.
   b. He's sleepy.
   c. He's sick.
   d. He's angry.
   e. It's hot.
   f. She's tired.
   g. She's old.
   h. They're thirsty.
   i. He's hungry.

2. Have students ask a question about each picture. (Is she busy? Is he tired?)

3. Have students answer "no" to each question. (Is she busy? No, she isn't busy.)

4. Pair students. Only one student uses the visual. Student asks his/her partner about each picture in random order.

C. THE FAMILY

1. Have students name the family members:

   a. Grandmother — Grandfather
   b. Daughter — Son
   c. Aunt — Uncle
   d. Mother-in-law — Father-in-law
   e. Mother — Father
   f. Sister — Brother
   g. Niece — Nephew — Cousin
   h. Sister-in-law — Brother-in-law

2. Arrange a family group in front of the room (similar to visual arrangement). With class members, assign roles (You're the father. You're the son. You're the daughter-in-law, etc.). Have the students identify themselves in relation to other members of the group.

D. MEALS AND SNACKS

1. Ask students: (1) When do you eat breakfast? Lunch? Dinner? When do you eat a snack? (2) What do you eat for breakfast? Lunch? Dinner?

2. Pair students. Have each student ask the other about meals and snacks.

E. WHY ISN'T SHE AT SCHOOL?

Ask questions from left column of the visual (Why isn't she at school? Why isn't he at work?). Students select an appropriate response. (*Example:* Because it's a holiday. Because he's sick.)

F. QUESTION WORDS

With students looking at the visual in the book or using an overhead transparency:

1. First, ask: *Who* is he? *What* is this? *When* do you come to school? *When* is your birthday? *Where* are they? *How* do you come to school? *Which* dress do you like? *Which* dress does your mother like? *Whose* ball is it? *Why* is English difficult?

2. Direct students to ask a question about number one or number four, etc. Question must begin with appropriate question word.

Supplemental Activities

A. PERSONAL INFORMATION AND INTRODUCTIONS

1. Pair the students. Have each introduce his/her partner to the class.

2. Direct students to turn to page 128 in Unit VII, Looking for a Job. Have students ask and answer (What's his occupation? He's a welder, etc.).

3. Write personal information questions on slips of paper. Each student draws one, reads the question, and answers it. Class may be divided into teams, and the team answering the most questions correctly wins.

B. STATES OF BEING/FEELINGS

1. Distribute several magazines to students. Have them work in groups to find pictures in the magazines to illustrate feelings or states of being. Have each group make a collage. (Provide butcher paper, scissors, glue.)

D. TELLING TIME

1. Have the students make individual clocks (with paper plates, one brad, two construction-paper clock hands). Instruct the class:

   a. Set the clock for 4:30, 6:15, etc.
   b. Show me when you wake up, eat lunch, etc.

2. Distribute free calendar booklets obtainable at card shops or gift stores. Start with January. Find any holidays. Have the students tell their birthdays. Proceed through the months. Have students tell the special dates celebrated in their countries.

Food and Money

COMPETENCY OBJECTIVES

On completion of this unit the students will show orally, in writing, or through demonstration that they are able to use the language needed to function in the following situations.

A. SHOPPING FOR FOOD

    1. Identify the most common foods.

    2. Ask for and locate foods.

    3. Use common tables of weights and measures.

    4. Differentiate between types of food stores—discount, supermarket, and 24-hour stores.

B. MONEY AND CHANGE

    1. Use American money.

    2. Ask for and make change.

C. EATING OUT

    1. Order from a menu.

    2. Know how to tip.

Pre-Post Assessment

A. SHOPPING FOR FOOD

1. Using the Fruits, Vegetables, Seafoods, Meat, and Poultry visuals, have the students identify the foods.

2. Have the students role-play a situation in which one student is a grocery store clerk and one is a customer. Customer asks the location of butter, carrots, fish. Clerk answers, using dairy section, produce section, meat department.

3. Using the Measurement visual, ask the students such questions as: How many ounces are in one pound? How many cups in a pint?

4. Write the names of a local discount store, supermarket, and convenience store on the board. Ask students where they shop and why. Which store is convenient? Cheap? Expensive?

B. MONEY AND CHANGE

Using actual or imitation money, students ask for change for a dollar, five dollars, ten dollars.

C. EATING OUT

Have students role-play a situation in which two play the part of a couple in a restaurant. They order a meal from the menu (Breakfast or Dinner Menu visual). A student playing the waitress takes the order. The couple talks about leaving a tip.

Let's Go To The Store

A. Let's go to the store on Saturday.
B. O.K. I need a lot of things.
A. Do you want to go to 7-Eleven, Safeway, or Fed-Mart?
B. Let's go to Fed-Mart. It's the cheapest.

PRACTICE

Let's go to the store.
      movies.
      park.

Let's go home.
      downtown.
      outside.

Let's go to school.
      church.
      Uptown Park.

I need a lot of things.
      many
      several
      a few
      a couple of

Food is cheap at Safeway.
Butter is cheaper at Ralph's.
Meat is cheapest at Fed-Mart.

A Convenient Store

A. Run to the store for a loaf of bread, please.
B. Which store?
A. Speedee Mart. It's fast and convenient.
B. All right. I'll be right back.

PRACTICE

Run to the store for bread.
              milk.
              fruit.

Which store is fast?
               open?
               convenient?

What Do We Need?

A. What do we need at the store?
B. We need a quart of milk, a pound of coffee, and a head of lettuce.
A. Do we need any eggs?
B. Yes, please get some.

PRACTICE

We need a pint of . . .
      a quart of . . .
      a gallon of . . .
      a liter of . . .

I have some coffee.
        sugar
        butter.
        milk.

I don't have any coffee.
          bread.
          rice.

Measurements:

  a loaf of
  a cube of
  a can of
  a pound of
  a kilo of
  a box of
  a package of
  a bottle of
  a sack of

SUPER! SALE!

NOW IN PROGRESS!
AT THE
GOLDEN CARROT
SUPERMART

EXTRA LEAN
GROUND BEEF
$ **1.39**

GOLDEN DELICIOUS
APPLES
1 lb. **29** ¢

AVOCADOS ----- EA. 39¢
PEARS ------- lb. 29¢
LETTUCE ------ EA. 29¢
STRAWBERRIES ---- lb. 49¢

SNAPPY CRUNCH ----- 49¢
SMILE TOOTHPASTE --- 67¢
WHIFF DEODORANT --- 89¢
BRIBE BRAND COOKIES --- 59¢
NATHANIEL ORANGE JUICE -- 72¢

LARGE
GRADE A
EGGS
1 DOZEN **59** ¢

STORE HOURS:
MON-FRI.
10 to 9 P.M.
SAT+SUN.
10 to 6

USDA
GRADE A
FRYER
FRESH + PAN-READY
69 ¢

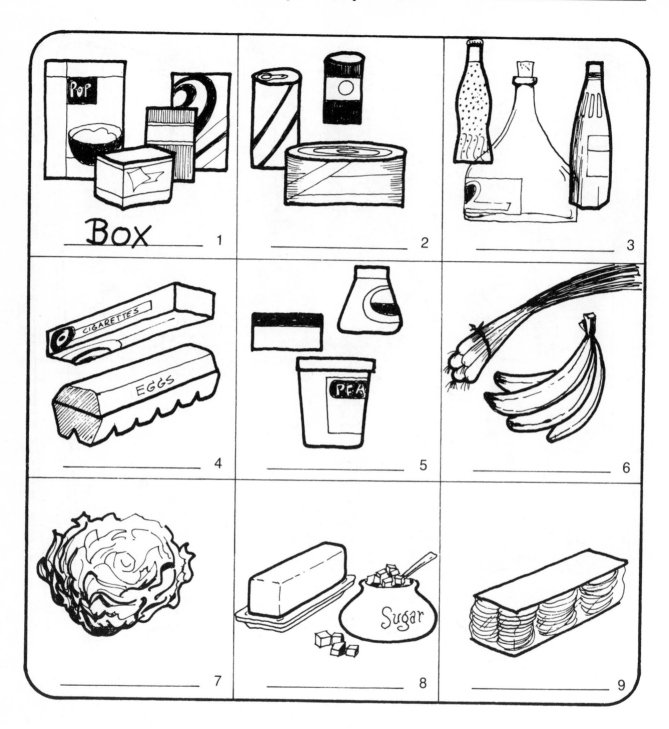

Box _____ 1

_____ 2

_____ 3

_____ 4

_____ 5

_____ 6

_____ 7

_____ 8

_____ 9

Where's The Milk?

A. Excuse me. Where's the milk?
B. It's in the dairy section at the end of aisle 8.
A. Thank you. I need several things from the dairy section.

PRACTICE

Where is the milk?
       butter?
       cottage cheese?
       cream?
       meat?
       shampoo?
       soda pop?
       peanut butter?

Where are the eggs?
       vegetables and fruit?
       paper towels?
       frozen foods?

It's in the bakery section.
       meat department.
       produce section.
       dairy section.
       paper goods section.

Buying Fish

A. How much is that fish?
B. It's 79¢ a pound. Do you want this one?
   It weighs two pounds.
A. Yes, I'll take it.
B. Is that all?
A. Yes, that's all today.

PRACTICE

How much is the fish?
       coffee?
       roast?

How much is the fish?
How much does the fish cost?
What is the price of the fish?

How much are the oranges?
       eggs?
       rolls?

We Need Bread

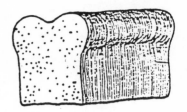

A. How much bread do we have?

B. One loaf. How many loaves do we need?

A. At least two. I need to make sandwiches for the picnic.

PRACTICE

How much bread do we have?
    milk
    coffee
    sugar

How many loaves of bread do we need?
    quarts of milk
    pounds of coffee
    pounds of sugar

Not Enough Milk

A. Oh, no. I don't have enough milk.

B. How much do you need?

A. I have one cup, but I need a pint.

B. I can go next door and borrow some.

PRACTICE

I don't have enough milk.
    bread.
    cheese.

I can go next door.
    to the store.
    borrow some.

8 OZ.
CUP

16 OZ.
1 PINT

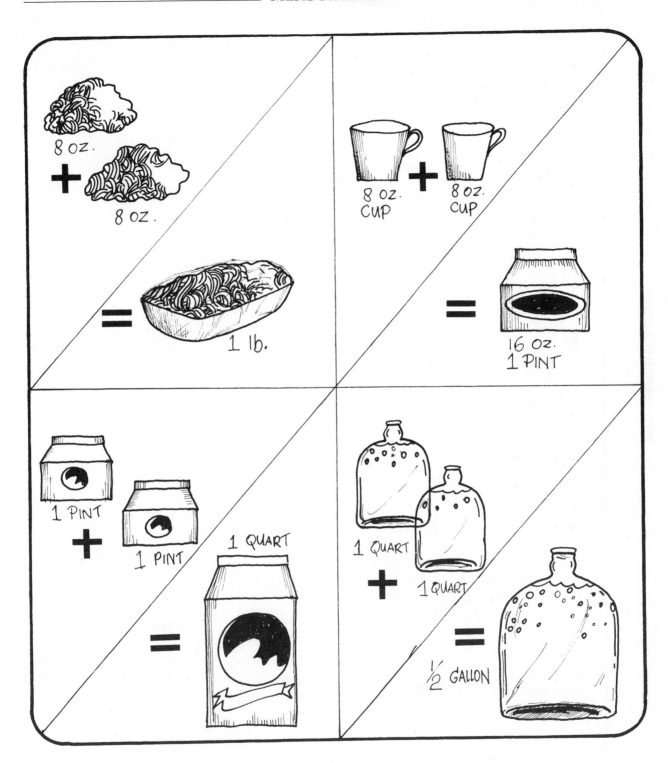

8 oz.

+

8 oz.

=

1 lb.

8 oz. CUP

+

8 oz. CUP

=

16 oz. 1 PINT

1 PINT

+

1 PINT

=

1 QUART

1 QUART

+

1 QUART

=

½ GALLON

FRUITS

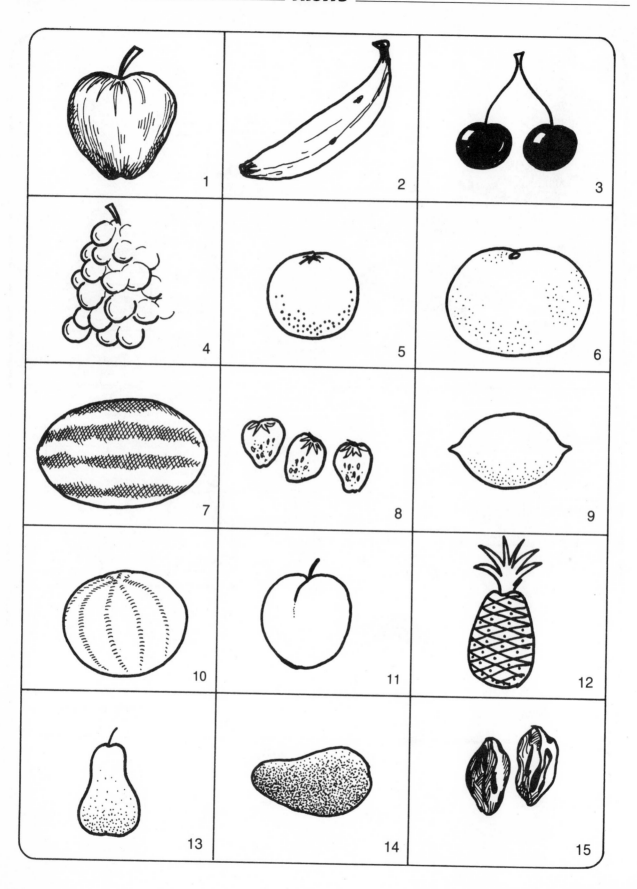

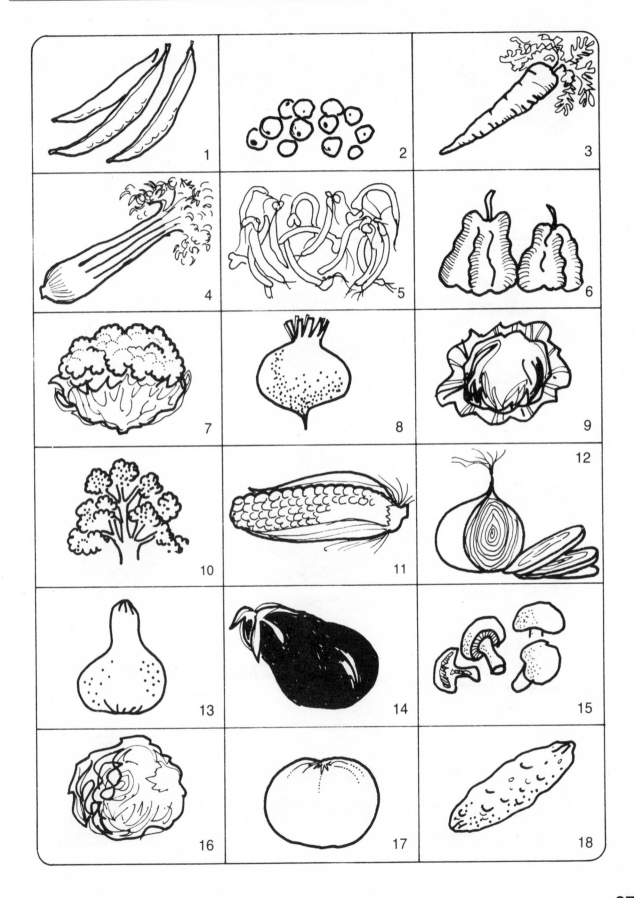

SEAFOOD

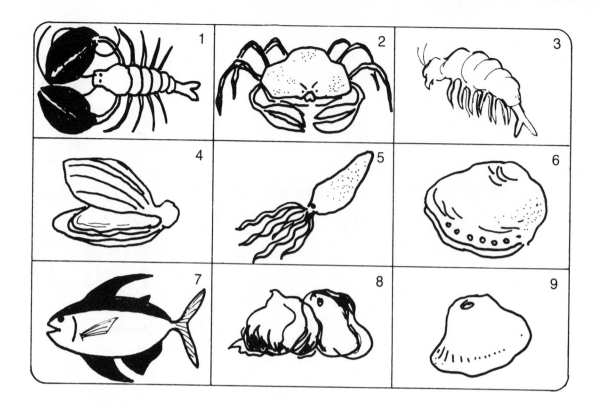

MEAT

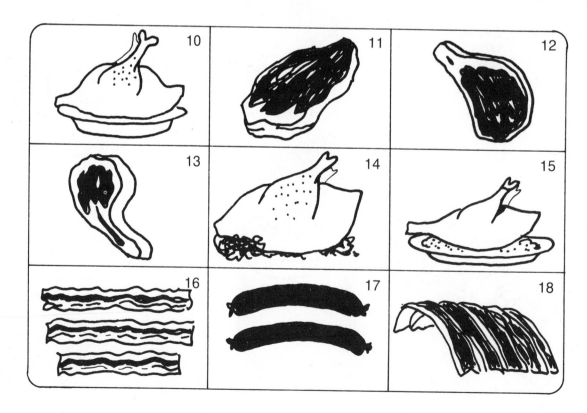

Making Change

A. Do you have change for a dollar?
   I want to buy a soft drink.

B. Here you are—50, 75, 85, 95, a dollar.

A. Thank you.

B. Use this machine. That one is out of order.

PRACTICE

Do you have change for a quarter?
                           a dollar?
                           5 dollars?
                           20 dollars?

I want to buy a soft drink.
                         a soda.
                         coffee.
                         tea.

That one is out of order.
                       not working.

Eating Out

A. May I see a menu, please?

B. Here you are. I'll be back in a minute to take your order.

A. Thank you.

PRACTICE

I'll be back in a minute.
           moment.

May I see a menu, please?
      have more coffee, please?
      have the check, please?

At The Restaurant

A. May I take your order, please?

B. Yes, I'd like some scrambled eggs and ham.

A. What would you like to drink?

B. Coffee, please.

A. Sugar and cream?

B. No, just black.

PRACTICE

What would you like to eat?
              to drink?
              for dessert?

I'd like scrambled eggs.
I'll have

Tipping

A. How much tip should I leave?
B. How much is the bill?
A. It's $4.00.
B. I usually tip 15%.
A. Okay. I'll leave 60¢.

PRACTICE

I usually tip 15%.
  frequently
  always
  generally

I'll leave the tip.
       a $5.00 tip.
  pay the bill.

HOW MUCH TIP WOULD YOU LEAVE?

GINO'S	
2 spaghetti	5.00
1 cheese pizza	2.50
4 orange sodas	2.00
	9.50
tax	.57
TOTAL	10.07

LUCY'S LUNCH	
4 egg salad	4.00
1 tuna melt	1.25
2 coffee	.90
2 tea	.90
	7.05
tax	.43
TOTAL	7.48

TOM'S CAFE	
2 hamb.	1.60
2 fries	1.00
2 coffee	.90
	3.50
tax	.21
TOTAL	3.71

BREAKFAST MENU

(The following breakfasts include toast, jelly, and hashed-brown potatoes.)

1 — Scrambled eggs 1.85

2 — 2 large fried eggs 1.95

3 — 1 large fried egg 1.50

4 — French toast 1.30

5 — 3 pancakes 1.25

6 — Ham and cheese omelette 1.75

Side Orders: Bacon .... .85
or
sausage

Sweet roll .... .45

Hot or cold cereal .... .60

Donut .... .30

Juices: Grapefruit .... .40   large .... .55

Orange .... .40   large .... .55

Tomato .... .35   large .... .50

Beverages: Coffee .... .25

Tea .... .25

Milk .... .30

Hot chocolate 30

Coca-Cola .... .30

DINNER MENU

Appetizers: Shrimp cocktail 1.50
Assorted hors d'oeuvres 1.50
French onion soup .... .90
Clam chowder .... .90

A La Carte: Spaghetti dinner 2.50
Fried chicken 2.50
Broiled fish 3.00
Ham with pineapple 2.75
Cheeseburger and French fries 1.60

Dinners: The dinners are served with soup or salad, your choice of dressing—blue cheese, thousand island, or French, baked or French-fried potatoes, and bread and butter.

Fried chicken 2.90
Golden fried shrimp 3.35
Top sirloin steak 4.05
Roast turkey dinner 3.10
Broiled fish 3.50

Child's Plate: Hamburger patty, fried potatoes, and milk $1.50

Side Orders: Baked potato .... .50
Onion rings .... .75
Chef's salad bowl 1.50
Corn on the cob (in season) .... .75

Desserts: Pie .... .70
Cake .... .70
Pudding, vanilla or chocolate .... .50
Ice cream or sherbert .... .45
Hot fudge sundae .... .90
Strawberry shortcake .... .85

Beverages: Coffee .... .25
Tea .... .25
Milk .... .30
Coca Cola .... .30   large .... .40
7-Up .... .30   large .... .40
Beer .... .50
Iced Tea .... .35

Every week Mrs. Lee goes to the supermarket. She buys a lot of things. She always buys a quart of milk, a dozen eggs, and a loaf of bread. Sometimes she needs a pound of coffee. If she doesn't have any flour or rice, she buys them. She goes to the bakery section for bread. She goes to the dairy section for milk and butter. She goes to the produce section for lettuce and tomatoes.

Questions

1. Where does Mrs. Lee go every week?
2. What does she always buy?
3. Where does she go for bread?
4. Where does she go for lettuce and tomatoes?

Write the Word

1. She _____ a lot of things.

2. She always buys a _____ of milk.

3. She always buys a _____ eggs.

4. She always buys a _____ of bread.

5. If she doesn't have any rice or flour, she buys _____.

6. She goes to the bakery section for _____.

7. She goes to the produce sections for _____ and

_____.

Write About You

1. Do you go to the supermarket every week? _____

_____

2. Which store do you go to? _____

_____

3. What do you always buy? _____

_____

4. Do you buy milk, eggs, and coffee? _____

_____

5. Where do you go for bread? _____

_____.

6. Do you need rice today? _____

_____.

READING EXERCISE—EATING OUT

     Sometimes the Lee family eats dinner in a restaurant. The waitress gives them a menu. In a few minutes, she comes back to take their order. She says, "May I take your order, please?" Mrs. Lee often orders fish, but her husband always orders steak. The waitress asks them what they would like to drink. Mrs. Lee generally drinks black coffee. Her husband frequently drinks a glass of wine. After dinner, the waitress brings them their bill. They seldom have dessert. They're too full! They always leave a tip for the waitress. They usually tip 15%. Eating out is fun!

Questions

1. What does the waitress give them first in the restaurant?
2. What do they order?
3. What does Mrs. Lee generally drink?
4. Do they usually have dessert?
5. What do they leave for the waitress?

Write the Word

1. The waitress brings them a _____.

2. The waitress takes their _____.

3. The waitress asks them what they would _____to drink.

4. Mrs. Lee _____drinks black coffee.

5. They _____have dessert.

6. They're too _____.

7. They always leave a _____.

8. They usually tip _____.

Write About You

1. Do you eat dinner in a restaurant? _____.

2. What do you usually order? _____

   _____.

3. What do you like to drink? _____

   _____.

4. Do you like dessert? _____

   _____.

5. Do you like to eat dinner in a restaurant or do you like to cook dinner at home? _____

   _____.

Using the Visuals

A. A SUPERMARKET AD

1. With each student looking at the visual or using an overhead transparency, ask such questions as:

   a. What are the weekday store hours?
   b. What are the weekend hours?
   c. How much is a head of lettuce?
   d. How much is a dozen eggs?
   e. How much is a pound of apples, etc.?

B. A BOX, A CAN, A BUNCH

1. With students looking at the visual or using an overhead transparency, ask them to identify the following:

   a. A box of cereal
   b. A can of tuna, soup, juice
   c. A bottle of soda, catsup, oil
   d. A carton of cigarettes, eggs
   e. A jar of peanut butter, mustard
   f. A bunch of green onions, bananas
   g. A head of lettuce
   h. A cube of butter, sugar
   i. A dozen cookies

C. WHAT'S IN THE REFRIGERATOR?

1. Have the students tell what food items are in each location.

   Key:

   a. Freezer—ice, ice cream, meat
   b. First shelf—milk, orange juice, wine
   c. Second shelf—oranges, yogurt, cottage cheese
   d. Third shelf—pineapple
   e. First door-shelf—salad dressings
   f. Second door-shelf—butter
   g. Third door-shelf—eggs
   h. Fourth door-shelf—mustard, jam

2. Then ask students at random where certain items are. Have more able students ask, also.

3. Next, ask questions such as, "What's between the oranges and cottage cheese? What's to the right of the orange juice?" etc.

4. If possible, make a paired visual (two copies) of "The Inside of the Refrigerator"— an "A" and a "B." In "A" delete (cover) several items (ice, yogurt, eggs, carrots). In "B" delete other items (ice cream, cottage cheese, orange juice, mustard).

   Pair the students. Students holding the "A" visual use this set of questions, and ask students with the "B" visual:

   a. Where's the ice?
   b. Where's the yogurt?
   c. Where are the eggs?
   d. Where are the carrots?

   "B" holders respond (It's in the freezer on the left). "A" holders write or draw the items in the appropriate locations.

   Students holding "B" visual use this set of questions:

   a. Where's the ice cream?
   b. Where's the cottage cheese?
   c. Where's the orange juice?
   d. Where's the mustard?

   On completion, students compare visuals to check accuracy of placement.

D. THE SUPERMARKET

1. Ask such questions as:

   a. Where is the cashier? (Near the cash register.)
   b. Who is loading the groceries? (Courtesy clerk.)
   c. What is the stock boy doing? (Restocking/putting out more oranges.)
   d. How many shopping carts do you see?
   e. Who is paying for the groceries?

E. MEASUREMENT

1. Ask the following questions:

   a. How many ounces in a pound?
   b. How many cups in a pint?
   c. How many pints in a quart?
   d. How many quarts in a gallon?

F. FRUITS, VEGETABLES, SEAFOOD, AND POULTRY

1. Have the students identify the foods:

   Key:

   a. Fruit — apple, banana, cherries, grapes, orange, grapefruit, watermelon, strawberries, lemon, cantaloupe, plum, pineapple, pear, avocado, dates
   b. Vegetables — green beans, peas, carrot, celery, bean sprouts, green peppers, cauliflower, beet, lettuce, broccoli, corn, onion, squash, eggplant, mushrooms, cabbage, tomato, cucumber
   c. Seafood — lobster, crab, shrimp, clam, squid, abalone, tuna, oyster, scallop
   d. Meat and Poultry — chicken, roast beef, pork chop, lamb chop, turkey, duck, bacon, sausage, spare ribs

2. Have students identify foods by making statements such as:

   a. I like apples.
   b. I don't like dates.
   c. I need some carrots.
   d. I don't need any onions.
   e. I have some fish.
   f. I don't have any chicken.

   or

   a. In my country we have _____.
   b. In my country we don't have _____.

G. BREAKFAST MENU, DINNER MENU

Role-play ordering from the menus in a restaurant. Have small groups come to the front of the room and practice ordering from the assigned waitress. Then break the class into small groups for additional practice. Circulate as you check on students' progress.

Supplemental Activities

A. SHOPPING FOR FOOD

1. Collect empty containers of common foods. Plastic fruits and vegetables are useful also.

   a. Have the students put the foods into proper categories—dairy products, packaged goods, canned foods, produce.
   b. Ask the students to hand someone a *jar* of mayonnaise, a *can* of tuna, a *package* of rice, a *box* of cereal.
   c. Have the students make a list of what they need at the store. Write the words on the board if needed.
   d. If possible, set up a store using a few classroom tables. Number the aisles. Have the students ask the clerk the location of foods.

B. MONEY AND CHANGE AND   C. EATING OUT

1. Using real or imitation money, pair the students as customers and cashiers. Have each customer pay a certain amount and the cashier make change.

2. Using the "checks" at the bottom of page 41, have the students decide how much tip they would leave. Discuss tipping customs in native countries.

Health Care

COMPETENCY OBJECTIVES

On completion of this unit the students will show orally, in writing, or through demonstration that they are able to use the language needed to function in the following situations.

A. PARTS OF THE BODY

    1. Identify parts of the body.

    2. Describe common health problems.

B. MEDICAL AND DENTAL APPOINTMENTS

    1. Make medical and dental appointments.

    2. Fill out basic medical forms.

C. PRESCRIPTIONS AND MEDICAL DOSAGES

    Follow directions for dosages on prescriptions.

D. EMERGENCY SITUATIONS

    Make emergency calls to proper agencies (police, fire department).

Pre-Post Assessment

A. PARTS OF THE BODY

    1. Looking at The Body visual but covering up the printed names, have the students identify the body parts.

    2. Looking at the What's the Matter visual, have the students describe each health problem.

B. MEDICAL AND DENTAL APPOINTMENTS

    1. Have the students role-play telephoning the doctor or dentist to make an appointment.

    2. Have the students fill out the Health Examination Record.

C. PRESCRIPTIONS AND MEDICAL DOSAGES

Using the Prescriptions visual, have the students explain the dosage amount and frequency.

D. EMERGENCY SITUATIONS

Have the students role-play calling police and fire stations in an emergency.

What's the Matter?

A. What's the matter?
B. My ankle hurts.
A. Oh, that's too bad.
   What happened?
B. I twisted it.

PRACTICE

My ankle hurts.
    foot
    hand
    head

I twisted it yesterday.
  cut
  broke
  hurt
  sprained

What's the matter?
What's the problem?
What's wrong?
What did you do?
What happened?

I have a headache.
        toothache.
        backache.
        stomachache.
    an earache.
    an infection.

I have a backache.
I have a pain in my back.
I have a sore back.
My back hurts.

How Do You Feel?

A. How do you feel?

B. So-So.

A. What's wrong?
   Do you have a fever?

B. No, I don't.
   I have a cold, and a bad cough.

A. You need some medicine for your throat.

B. You're right. I'll get some.

PRACTICE

Do you have a fever?
            cold?
            cough?
            sore throat?
            the flu?

You need some medicine for your throat.
                              fever.
                              cold.

Where Were You Yesterday?

A. Where were you yesterday?
   We missed you.

B. I was sick and stayed home.

A. Were your children sick, too?

B. Yes, but we're all fine today.

PRACTICE

I was sick yesterday.
You were sick yesterday.
He/She was sick yesterday.

We were sick
You were
They were

Where were you?
Where was he/she/it?
Where were they?

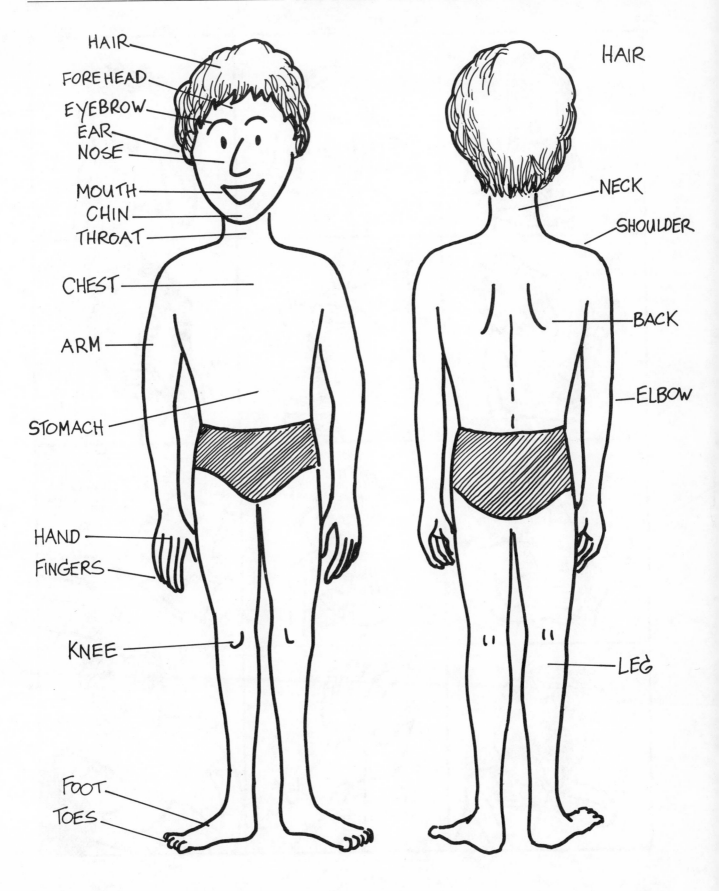

HAIR
FOREHEAD
EYEBROW
EAR
NOSE
MOUTH
CHIN
THROAT
CHEST
ARM
STOMACH
HAND
FINGERS
KNEE
FOOT
TOES

HAIR
NECK
SHOULDER
BACK
ELBOW
LEG

I Have An Appointment

A. My name is Joe Garcia.
   I have a 3:15 appointment with Dr. Brown.
B. You're a new patient, aren't you?
A. Yes, I am.
B. Please fill out this form, then the doctor will see you.

PRACTICE

You're a new patient, aren't you?
He's   isn't he?
She's   isn't she?

We're   new patients, aren't we?
You're   aren't you?
They're   aren't they?

Please fill out this form.
            fill in   health form.
            complete paper.

Calling The Doctor

A. Hello, Dr. Green's office.
B. This is Mary Thompson.
   I'm calling about my daughter, Sarah.
   She has a fever and a rash.
A. When can you bring her in?
B. Right away.
A. All right. We'll see you in a few minutes.

PRACTICE

I'm calling about my daughter.
You're calling   your
He's calling   his
She's calling   her

We're calling   our
They're calling   their

I can bring her in right now.
                   right away.
                   at once.
                   immediately.

Making An Appointment

A. I want to make an appointment with Dr. Brown.
B. Who's calling please?
A. Mary Park.
B. Are you a new patient?
A. Yes, I am. I need a physical for a new job.
B. Can you come in on Thursday at 2:30?
A. Yes, I can. Thank you.

PRACTICE

I want to make an appointment.
   need
   have

I need a physical.
   physical exam.
   physical examination.
   checkup.

Robert Gann, M.D.
Name *Anne Howard*
Appointment date: _____
   Thurs. 9-28
Time: _____ *10:45 a.m.*

Dr. Jane Lee
Name *Susan Lane*
Next appt: _____
   Tues. 6-18
Time: _____ *9:20 a.m.*

Dr. Bill Brown
Name *Tom Jones*
Next appointment:
   Fri. April 16
Time: _____ *2:30 p.m.*

STANDARD HEALTH EXAMINATION RECORD

Date ___ / ___ / ___
    mo day year

Name _____ _____
         (last)   (first)

Age _____ Sex _____

Address _____ Phone _____ Birthdate _____

MEDICAL HISTORY

Have you had any problems with:
(check ✔)

PAST ILLNESSES

Frequent colds _____
Frequent sore throats _____
Bronchitis _____
Allergies _____
Operations or serious
    injuries _____
Stomach upsets _____
Kidney trouble _____
Convulsions _____
Tuberculosis _____
Diabetes _____
Blood diseases (anemia, etc) _____
High blood pressure _____
Heart attacks _____
Mental depression _____
Bad headaches or migraines _____
Liver trouble (hepatitis) _____

DISEASES

Chicken pox _____
Measles _____
Mumps _____
Scarlet Fever _____
Poliomyelitis _____
Whooping Cough _____
Other _____

SURGERIES   DATE

_____   _____
_____   _____
_____   _____
_____   _____

IMMUNIZATIONS—TESTS

Diphtheria _____
Whooping Cough _____
Poliomyelitis _____
Tetanus _____
Smallpox _____
Typhoid _____
Tuberculin _____
Other _____

List of Medications You Are Now
    Taking

_____
_____
_____

Allergies to Medications

_____
_____

1. What is this temperature?

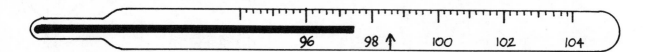

2. What is this temperature?

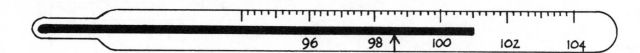

3. Show a *normal* adult temperature on the thermometer below.

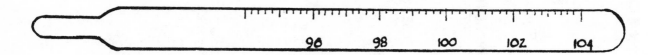

4. Show a temperature of 101.2° on this thermometer.

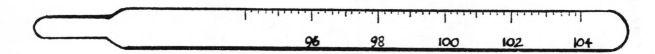

Seeing The Dentist

A. I have a very bad toothache.
B. You need to see the dentist.
   Didn't you make an appointment?
A. Yes, I did.
   I'm going to see Dr. Green this afternoon at 4:00.
B. Oh, that's good. He's a good dentist.

PRACTICE

Did you need to see the dentist?
Did he   doctor?
Did she

Did we
Did you
Did they

Yes, I did.
Yes, you
Yes, he
Yes, she
Yes, it

Yes, we did.
Yes, you
Yes, they

Didn't you make an appointment?
Didn't he/she

Didn't we
Didn't they

No, I didn't.
No, you
No, he
No, she
No, it

No, we didn't.
No,
No,

The Drugstore

A. Is my prescription ready?

B. Yes, here it is.

A. How much should I take?

B. One pill every four hours.
   The directions are on the label.

A. Thanks a lot.

B. You're welcome. Have a nice day.

PRACTICE

Take one pill every four hours.
              before meals.
         capsule after meals.
         tablet as needed for pain.
Take no more than four daily.

How much should I take?

One teaspoon at bedtime.
              three times a day.
              twice a day.
              once a day.

How many should I take?

Two pills twice a day.
         at bedtime.

Cough Medicine

A. Do you have cough medicine?

B. Yes, we do. Here's a good one.

A. How much is it?

B. I have two sizes.
   The big bottle is $5.00.
   The small one is $3.00.

A. O.K. I'll take the small one.

PRACTICE

Do you have cough medicine?
              syrup?
              drops?
              lozenges?

I'll take this one.
I'll take that one.

I'll take these.
I'll take those.

FED-MART PHARMACY

3249 Sports Arena Blvd.

No. 623,451   224-3683

Dr. William Anderson

Than Nguyen   2/6/79
One tablet before meals.

DRUG MART

3056 Clairemont Drive

No. 536,120   276-2310

Dr. James Bond

Maria Garcia   6/2/79
Take two teaspoons every four hours
for cough.   REFILL

LONG'S DRUGS

953 5th St.

No. 563,122,321   232-4191

Dr. Mary White

Janet Smith   6/2/79
Put one drop in each eye
3 times a day.

THRIFTY DRUG STORE

4359 54th St.

No. 3216   583-0586

Dr. Sam Lee

Seiko Yamaiko   5/10/79
Take one capsule daily.

To get a prescription refilled, call the drugstore. Tell the druggist the number and date on the label. The druggist will call the doctor if necessary.

OVER-THE-COUNTER DRUGS

HOW TO USE MEDICINE

Keep lid tightly closed.
Keep out of reach of children.
Shake before using.
Avoid excessive heat.
Do not exceed recommended dosage.
May cause drowsiness.
If symptoms persist, consult physician.

A-1 COLD TABLETS

Dosage: 2 tablets to start, followed by 1 tablet every 4 hours, not to exceed 4 tablets daily.

Children: 6–12—One-half adult dosage

Continue treatment for 72 hours.

TIME CAPSULES

Dosage: 1 capsule every 12 hours.
One capsule in the morning and one capsule at bedtime.

CAUTION: Children under 12 use only as directed by physician.

ALPHA-SELTZER.

Must be dissolved before taking.

Adults: 1 or 2 tablets in water. Repeat as needed, up to 8 tablets dissolved in ¼ glass of warm water.

Children: ½ adult dosage.

CAUTION: For children under 3, consult your physician.

1-WAY NASAL SPRAY

Adults: Spray once or twice in each nostril.

Children: Spray once.

Children under 6: Consult physician. Repeat in 3 to 4 hours if necessary.

PEPTO-BISMARCK

Adults: 2 tablespoonfuls

Children: According to age:
10–14 years—4 teaspoonfuls
6–10 years—2 teaspoonfuls
3– 6 years—1 teaspoonful

Repeat above dosage every ½ to 1 hour, if needed, or until 7 or 8 doses are taken.

COUGH SYRUP

Adults: 1 to 2 teaspoonfuls.

Children: 6–12 years—½ to 1 teaspoonful.
2–6 years—½ teaspoonful.

May be repeated in 4 hours, if necessary, but not more than 4 times in 24 hours.

FLIP'S MILK OF MAGNESIA

Adults: As an antacid—1 to 4 teaspoonfuls with a little water.

As a laxative—2 to 4 tablespoonfuls in a glass of water.

Children: ¼ to ½ of adult dose.

EYE DROPS

Squeeze 2 or more drops into each eye as often as desired. Replace cap. Do not touch dropper to any surface.

Emergency!

A. Operator.

B. This is an emergency!
   I need help!
   Someone is choking!

A. I'll connect you
   with the police department.
   They will send a police ambulance.

PRACTICE

Get me the police!
        fire department!
        sheriff!
        poison center!
    an ambulance!

Someone is choking.
        bleeding.
        unconscious.
        burned.
        hurt.

Police Ambulance

A. Police department.

B. Someone is choking!
   Please send a police ambulance!

A. Where are you?

B. I'm at 1753 Fifth Avenue.

A. What is your name, please?

B. Bill Lee.

A. The ambulance will come immediately.
   Goodbye.

EMERGENCY TELEPHONE NUMBERS

Write in the numbers for the city you live in.

POLICE _____

FIRE DEPARTMENT _____

HIGHWAY PATROL _____

WEATHER _____

TELEGRAMS _____

COUNTY SHERIFF _____

For assistance or dialing instructions: **Dial Operator ("O"). In any emergency: Dial Operator ("O").**

For emergency calls to other counties and states: **Dial Operator and give the name and address of the agency you wish to call.**

Yesterday Mrs. Lee was sick and stayed home. She had a cold and a bad cough. She needed some medicine for her sore throat. Her daughter was sick, too. Mrs. Lee took her daughter's temperature. It was 100°! She had a fever. Mrs. Lee called the doctor. He told her to bring her daughter in. Then he wrote a prescription for medicine. Mrs. Lee went to the drugstore to get it. The label said, "Take one pill every four hours." She always reads the label carefully. She also bought some medicine for her sore throat. Both Mrs. Lee and her daughter feel fine now.

Questions

1. How was Mrs. Lee yesterday?
2. Was her daughter sick, too?
3. What was her temperature?
4. How did the doctor help her?

Write the Word

1. Yesterday Mrs. Lee needed some medicine for her _____.

2. She took her daughter's _____. It was 100°.

3. She had a _____.

4. The doctor wrote a _____ for medicine.

Write About You

1. Are you sick today? _____

2. Were you sick yesterday? _____

3. Did you stay home? _____

_____

4. Do you have a sore throat? _____

_____

5. What do you buy at the drugstore? _____

_____

6. Do you read the labels on your medicine? _____

_____

Using the Visuals

A. PARTS OF THE BODY

1. After the students can name the body parts from the visual, instruct students to:

   a. Touch your face.
   b. Bend your elbow.
   c. Shake your arm.
   d. Scratch your ear.
   e. Rub your chin, etc.

B. WHAT'S THE MATTER?

1. Have the students describe each health problem:

   Key:

   a. She has a headache.
   b. He has a toothache.
   c. He has an earache.
   d. He has a stomachache.
   e. She has a backache.
   f. She has a cold/the flu.
   g. She has the measles/a rash.
   h. He has a broken arm.
   i. He has a fever.
   j. He's choking.
   k. He's bleeding.
   l. She's unconscious. She fainted.

2. Pair the students. One student asks, "What's the matter?" the other student tells about an illness.

C. TAKING PRESCRIPTION MEDICINE

1. Have the students identify the doctor.

2. Name the pharmacy (drugstore).

3. Tell the patient's name.

4. Give the dosage and frequency.

D. OVER-THE-COUNTER DRUGS

Read the directions, or have students carefully read the directions. Where possible, have empty containers of nasal spray, eyedrops, teaspoon, etc. to demonstrate activity.

Supplemental Activities

A. PARTS OF THE BODY AND   B. MEDICAL AND DENTAL APPOINTMENTS

1. Role-play calling the doctor's or dentist's office to make an appointment for (a) a physical exam, (b) an illness, (c) a dental appointment.

2. Refer to the appointment cards at the bottom of the Making An Appointment dialogue on page 56. Ask such questions as:

   a. When is Anne Howard's appointment?
   b. Who has an appointment with Dr. Lee?
   c. Who is Tom Jones' doctor?
   d. What time is Susan Lane's appointment?

C. PRESCRIPTION AND MEDICAL DOSAGES

Role-play asking the pharmacist (druggist) for medication for a cold. Discuss cold remedies used in native countries.

D. EMERGENCY SITUATIONS

1. Role-play calling the police in an emergency. Set up situations such as car accident, house burglary (robbery), lost child, etc.

2. Role-play calling the fire department in an emergency.

3. Make a pocket chart game of Concentration (memory), using emergency vocabulary (police, fire, emergency, ambulance, accident, help, burglar, prowler, etc). Then make eight pairs of cards with words on one side and numbers from 1 to 16 on the other. Set up the cards in the chart with the numbers showing. Student calls out any two numbers in an effort to match two words. When a match is made, student must use the word in a sentence. Then another student tries to make a match. (Cards could be made for any set of new vocabulary.)

4

Transportation

COMPETENCY OBJECTIVES

On completion of this unit the students will show orally, in writing, or through demonstration that they are able to use the language needed to function in the following situations.

A. LOCAL TRANSPORTATION

1. Use city buses to travel to school, shopping areas, jobs, and homes of friends.

2. Call a taxi when needed.

3. Walk safely in prescribed areas.

4. Buy gasoline at a service station and communicate simple needs to attendant.

B. OUT-OF-TOWN TRANSPORTATION

1. Buy a bus ticket to a designated city.

2. Differentiate between one-way and round-trip ticket.

3. Check and tag baggage.

Pre-Post Assessment

A. LOCAL TRANSPORTATION

　　1. Have the students role-play the following situations:

　　　　a. Asking for the fare, a schedule, and transfer on the city bus.
　　　　b. Calling for a taxi.
　　　　c. Crossing the street at an intersection.
　　　　d. Buying gasoline at a service station.

B. OUT-OF-TOWN TRANSPORTATION

　　1. Have the students role-play the following situations:

　　　　a. Buying a bus ticket to a nearby city.
　　　　b. Asking for a round-trip ticket.
　　　　c. Checking baggage.

I Walk To School

A. How do you come to school?

B. I walk. I live just around the corner.

A. Oh, I ride the bus.
I live a long way from here.

PRACTICE

I ride the bus.
  ride my bicycle.
  drive my car.

I come by bus.
          car.
          bicycle.
          skateboard.

I live a long way from here.
        around the corner.
        3 miles away.
        six blocks away.
        near here.
        near the park.

Cross At The Crosswalk

A. Don't cross in the middle of the street.

B. Why not?

A. It's dangerous. Maybe you'll get a ticket. Cross at the crosswalk.

B. O.K. Let's cross now. It says "WALK."

PRACTICE

Don't cross in the middle of the street.
          against the light.
          on a red light.
          when it says, "DON'T WALK."

Cross at the crosswalk.
      at the corner.
      on the green light.
      in the pedestrian crossing.

PED XING

Don't cross.	Why not?	It's dangerous.
Don't smoke.	Why not?	It's not allowed.
Don't cry.	Why not?	
Don't do that.	Why not?	

Taking The Bus

A. Watch your step, lady.
B. Does this bus go downtown?
A. Yes ma'am. Put your fare in the box.
B. How much is it?
A. It's 35¢. Exact change, please.

PRACTICE

Does this bus go downtown?
     to the border?
     to Mission Valley?
     to Ocean Beach?

How much is it?
What is the fare?

Bus Schedules

A. You're late today, driver.
B. No, I'm not, ma'am. We changed the schedule.
 This bus comes five minutes after every hour now.
 Here's a new schedule.
A. Oh, I see. Thank you very much.

PRACTICE

This bus comes 5 minutes after every hour.
     10   before
    every hour on the hour.
         half-hour.

Transfer, Please

A. How do I get to the West Side Shopping Area?

B. Take this bus downtown. Transfer to the number 34 bus at 4th and Broadway.

A. Does it cost more than 35¢.

B. No, give this transfer to the other driver.

A. Thank you very much. Please tell me where to change buses.

PRACTICE

How do I get to North Park?
               Mission Valley?
               the East Side?
               the beach?

Tell me where to change buses.
               catch the bus.
               get on the bus.
               get off the bus.

Calling A Taxi

A. Is this 234-6161?

B. Yes, this is Yellow Cab.

A. Please send a cab to 4030 Felton Street.

B. O.K. We'll send one right away.

A. Thank you.

PRACTICE

Please send a cab.
                    driver.
                    taxi.

We'll send one right away.
                    now.
                    immediately.
                    at once.

Using A Taxi

A. I want to go to 5th and Broadway. How much is the fare?

B. Well, that's about 5 miles. It's $1.20 for the first mile and 60¢ a mile after that.

A. That's fine. I have to get downtown in a hurry.

Fill It Up!

A. Fill it up with regular, please.

B. O.K. Should I check under the hood?

A. Please, and wash the windows, too.

B. Everything's fine under the hood.
That'll be $8.00.

A. Here you are. Thank you.

PRACTICE

Should I check under the hood?
     the water and oil?
     the tires?
     the battery?

O.K. Should I check under the hood?
  Do you want me to check under the hood?
  Is it necessary to check under the hood?

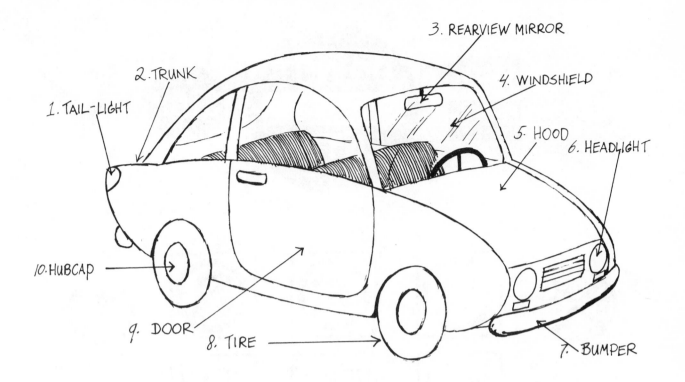

3. REARVIEW MIRROR

2. TRUNK

4. WINDSHIELD

1. TAIL-LIGHT

5. HOOD

6. HEADLIGHT

10. HUBCAP

9. DOOR

8. TIRE

7. BUMPER

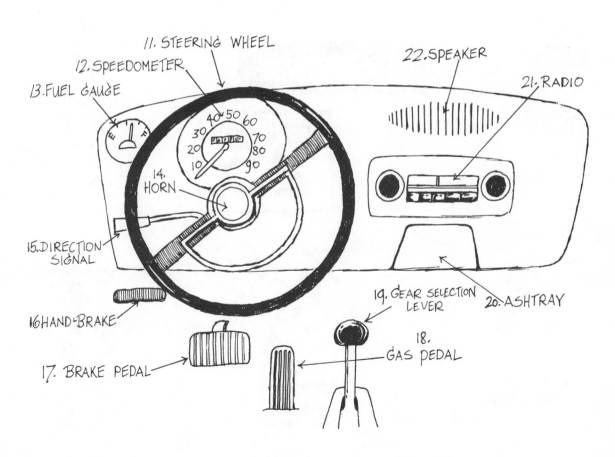

11. STEERING WHEEL

12. SPEEDOMETER

22. SPEAKER

13. FUEL GAUGE

21. RADIO

14. HORN

15. DIRECTION SIGNAL

19. GEAR SELECTION LEVER

20. ASHTRAY

16. HAND-BRAKE

18. GAS PEDAL

17. BRAKE PEDAL

1

WALK
DON'T WALK

2

DO NOT ENTER

3

STOP

4

YIELD

5

R X R

6

NO LEFT TURN

7

NO RIGHT TURN

8

NO U TURN

9

10

MEN WORKING

11

ONE WAY

12

SPEED LIMIT 25 MILES

13

ROAD CONSTRUCTION AHEAD

14

MERGE

15

SLIPPERY WHEN WET

16

TWO WAY TRAFFIC

17

_____

_____

_____

Match the Signs with the Meaning.

A. Two lanes go into one lane (merge).

B. Railroad crossing.

C. No U-turn.

D. Pedestrians cross here (people walk across the street).

E. Don't go. Stop.

F. Let other cars go first (yield).

_____

_____

_____

Packing A Suitcase

A. What are you doing?
B. I'm packing a suitcase.
   We're going to Garden Center.
A. What are you putting in there?
B. I'm taking a doll to my granddaughter.
A. When are you going?
B. I'm leaving now.

PRACTICE

I'm packing a suitcase.	What am I doing?
You're	are you
He's/She's	is he/she
We're	are we
They're	are you
	are they

I'd Like Two Tickets

A. May I help you?
B. Yes. How much is a ticket
   to Garden Center?
A. One-way or round-trip?
B. Round-trip.
A. It's $12.00 for round-trip.
B. O.K. I'd like two tickets,
   please.

PRACTICE

How much is a ticket?
         one-way ticket?
         round-trip ticket?

Checking The Bags

A. Where do we check the baggage?

B. At the end of the counter. We'll tag it there.

A. May I carry this on the bus?

B. Certainly. Claim your other bags in Garden Center.

PRACTICE

Where do we check the baggage?
                 luggage?
                 suitcases?

May I carry this on the bus?
       take   train?
                 airplane?

You get off in Garden Center.
       on   Harper Town.
      at 5th Avenue.
          College Avenue.
     downtown.

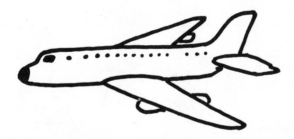

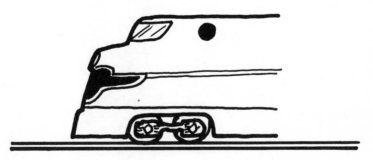

Ann comes to school by bus. She lives a long way from school. She waits for the bus at the bus stop. When she gets on the bus, she puts her fare in the box. The fare is 35¢. She has the exact change. Sometimes she goes downtown. Then she needs a transfer to change buses.

Questions

1. How does Ann come to school?
2. Where does she wait for the bus?
3. Where does she put the fare?
4. Why does she need a transfer?

Write the Word

1. Ann comes to school by _____.

2. She lives a _____ from school.

3. She puts her _____ in the box.

4. When she goes downtown, she gets a _____.

Write About You

1. How do you come to school? _____

_____

2. Do you live far from school? _____

_____

3. Do you ride a bicycle? _____

_____

4. Do you drive a car? _____

_____

Mrs. Brown is packing her suitcase now. She and her husband are going to Los Angeles. They're going to buy round-trip tickets. They will check their baggage at the ticket counter. After they get off the bus in Los Angeles, they will claim their baggage.

Questions

1. Where are Mr. and Mrs. Brown going?
2. What kind of tickets are they going to buy?
3. Where will they check their baggage?
4. Where will they claim their baggage?

Write the Word

1. Mrs. Brown is _____ her suitcase now.

2. Mr. and Mrs. Brown are going to buy _____ tickets.

3. They will check their _____ at the ticket counter.

4. After they get off in Los Angeles, they will _____ their baggage.

Write About You

1. Do you ride the bus? _____

_____

2. Where do you go? _____

_____

3. Do you pack your suitcase? _____

_____

4. What do you put in it? _____

_____

5. Do you check your baggage? _____

_____

Using The Visuals

A. THE CAR

   1. Have the students point to each part of the car as you say the name.

   2. Explain the concept of *inside* the car and *outside* the car. Say the name of a part, and ask the students to respond, telling you if the part is inside or outside.

   3. Pair the students. Have them ask one another the location of parts on the car.

B. ROAD SIGNS

Have students interpret the signs either orally or by demonstration.

Supplemental Activities

A. LOCAL TRANSPORTATION

   1. Have the students ask each other how far they live from school. Draw a school on the board.

      Set out large cards with "near, far from, around the corner, close to, a long way" written on them. Students select a location word and stand in the appropriate place.

   2. Pair the students. Have each student give directions to his or her home to a classmate.

   3. Take a suitcase to class (or pantomime this) and set up an imaginary situation, saying, "I'm going on a trip. In my suitcase I'm putting . . ."

      a. First time: have students put in articles of clothing. They must remember what previous students have said and add one more item.
      b. Second time: have students put in food items.
      c. Third time: have students put in furniture, etc.

   4. Have the students role-play the following situations:

      a. Getting on the bus, asking the fare, requesting a transfer and a schedule.
      b. Getting a ticket for jaywalking.
      c. Driving into a service station and getting gasoline.

   5. Complete the Reading Traffic Signs activity.

B. OUT-OF-TOWN TRANSPORTATION

   1. Assign more able students to telephone bus station, airport, or train station to obtain specified information.

   2. Have students practice roleplaying buying tickets for the bus, train, or airplane.

Housing

COMPETENCY OBJECTIVES

On completion of this unit the students will show orally, in writing, or through demonstration that they are able to use the language needed to function in the following situations.

A. LOCATING HOUSING

   1. Use classified ads to find suitable housing.

   2. State housing needs to potential landlords.

   3. Explain cleaning deposit arrangements.

B. IDENTIFYING ROOMS AND FURNISHINGS

   1. Name the rooms in a house or apartment.

   2. Name common household furniture.

C. APARTMENT REGULATIONS

Explain rules regarding pets, noise, etc. in an apartment complex.

D. MAINTENANCE PROBLEMS

   1. Describe repairs needed for maintenance.

   2. Identify common tools.

Pre-Post Assessment

A. LOCATING HOUSING

   1. Using the Housing Ads visual, ask the students:

      a. How much is the rent for the studio apartment?
      b. How much is the rent for the two-bedroom apartment?

   2. Have the students role-play the following situations:

      a. Renter asks landlord about apartment, number of rooms, rent.
      b. Landlord explains cleaning deposit to new tenant.

B. IDENTIFYING ROOMS AND FURNISHINGS

Using the Inside the House visual:

   1. Have the students identify the rooms.

   2. Have them identify the furnishings.

C. APARTMENT REGULATIONS

Using the Apartment Rules visual, have the students match the appropriate picture with each rule and explain it.

D. MAINTENANCE PROBLEMS

   1. Using the Housing Repairs visual, have the students tell about each problem.

   2. Using the Fixing Up the House and Yard visual, have the students identify the repair people and tell what each would be called to fix.

   3. Using the Tools visual, have the students name each tool, telling who would use each one.

Reading The Ads

A. Did you see this ad for an apartment on Iowa Street?
B. Yes, but I don't understand "near all."
A. It means it's close to school and shopping.
B. Oh, that's good. Let's go look it over.

> **$175**   Large 2 BR
> SHADY HOLLOW APTS.
> Incl. all utils & Cable TV, stove, refrig, disposal, drps, plush cpts, adjacent shopping, on a quiet, tree lined cul-de-sac w/off street parking, garages & carports avail. 1 child, no dogs. Near College & University, 583-2232

PRACTICE

I don't understand "near all."
                "w/w carpets."
                "util inc."
                "fencd yd."

It's close to schools.
                buses.
                downtown.
                churches.
                stores.

A Cleaning Deposit

A. How much is the rent for the two-bedroom apartment?
B. It's $175.00. You pay gas and lights. We pay water.
A. Do you require a cleaning deposit?
B. Yes, we require a $50.00 cleaning deposit. You get it back if the apartment is clean when you move out.
A. Thank you. We'll think about it.

PRACTICE

Do you require a cleaning deposit?
        need
        refund the

You pay gas and lights.
        utilities.
        the water bill.
        the cleaning deposit.

What's A Studio Apartment?

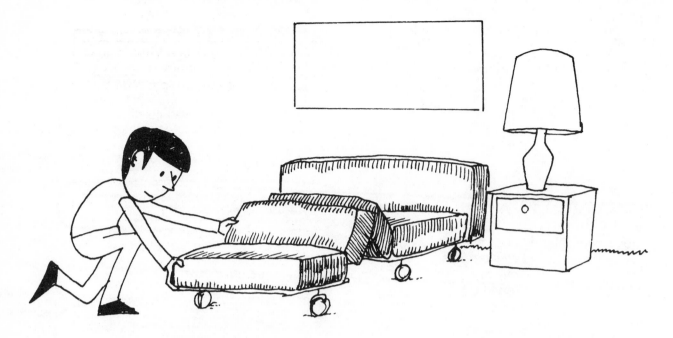

A. We need a one-bedroom apartment.

B. We don't have one, but our studio apartment is vacant.

A. What's a studio apartment?

B. It's one large room with a kitchen/dining area, a bathroom, and a couch that opens to make a bed.

A. Oh! How much is the rent?

B. $150 a month including utilities.

A. Let's look at it.

PRACTICE

A studio apartment is vacant.
                 empty.
                 available.

It has a kitchen.
        bathroom.
        dining room.
        living room.
        family room.
        large closet.
        garage.

We need a one-bedroom apartment.
        two-bedroom
        studio

What is—what's
Let us—let's

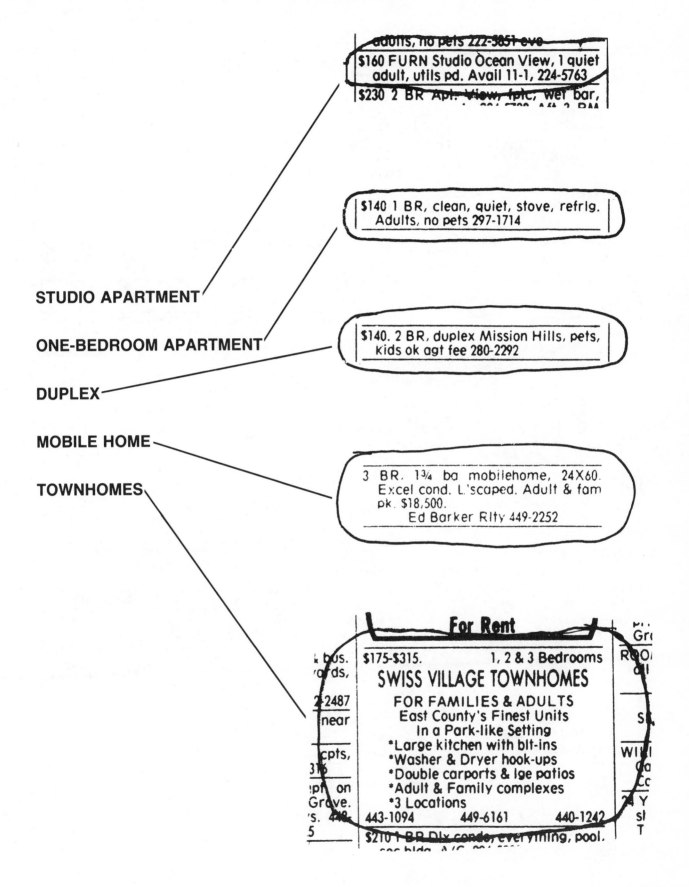

adults, no pets 222-3851 eve

$160 FURN Studio Ocean View, 1 quiet
adult, utils pd. Avail 11-1, 224-5763

$230 2 BR Apt. View, fplc, wet bar,

$140 1 BR, clean, quiet, stove, refrig.
Adults, no pets 297-1714

$140. 2 BR, duplex Mission Hills, pets,
kids ok agt fee 280-2292

3 BR, 1¾ ba mobilehome, 24X60.
Excel cond. L'scaped. Adult & fam
pk. $18,500.
Ed Barker Rlty 449-2252

STUDIO APARTMENT

ONE-BEDROOM APARTMENT

DUPLEX

MOBILE HOME

TOWNHOMES

For Rent

$175-$315.   1, 2 & 3 Bedrooms

SWISS VILLAGE TOWNHOMES

FOR FAMILIES & ADULTS
East County's Finest Units
In a Park-like Setting
*Large kitchen with blt-ins
*Washer & Dryer hook-ups
*Double carports & lge patios
*Adult & Family complexes
*3 Locations
443-1094   449-6161   440-1242

$210 1 BR Dlx condo, everything, pool.

APARTMENT

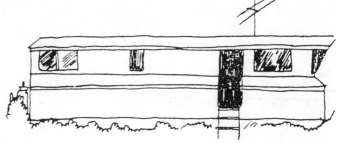

MOBILE HOME

HOUSE

TOWNHOUSE

DUPLEX

INSIDE THE HOUSE

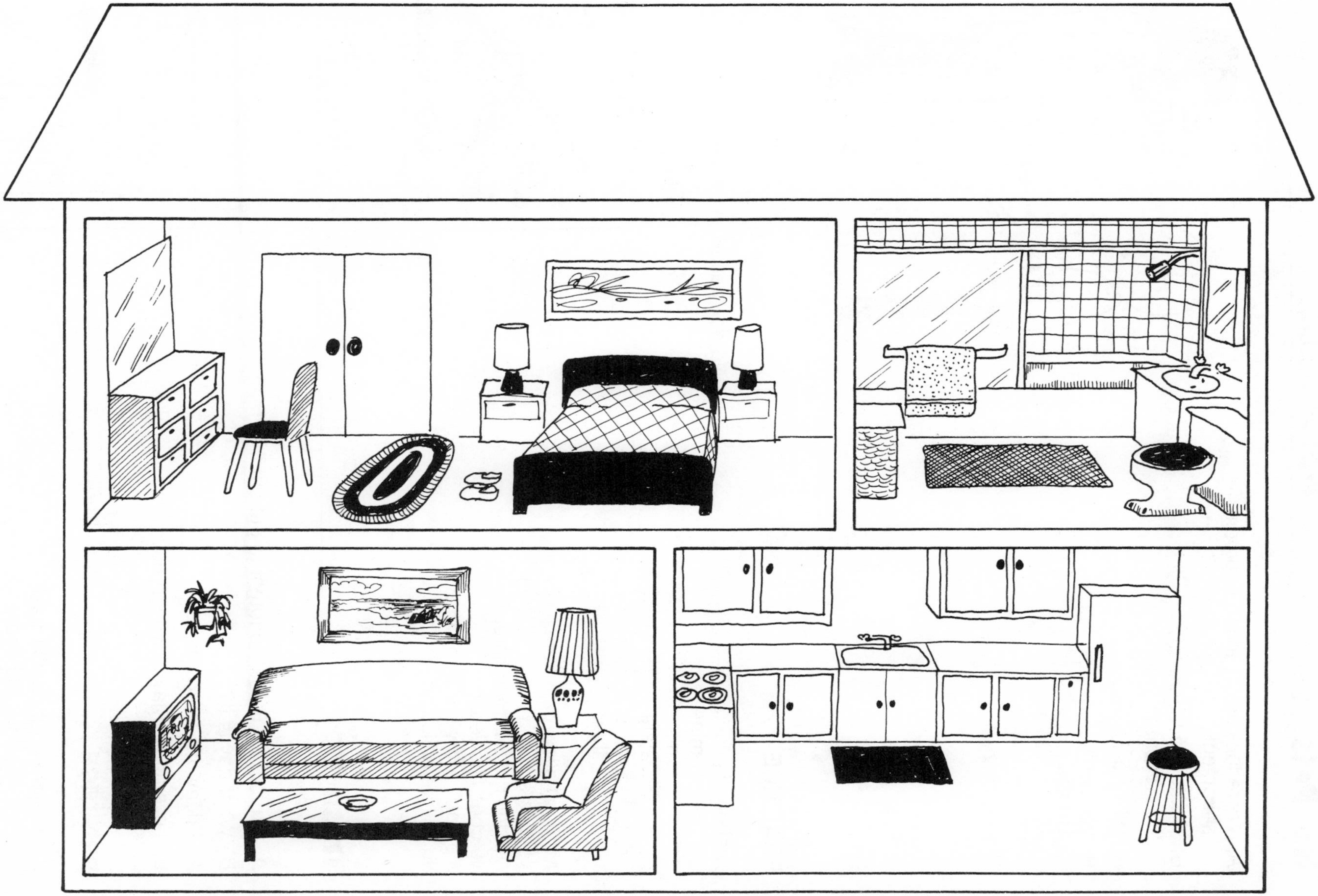

No Pets

A. We're looking for a one-bedroom apartment.

B. If that dog is yours, I can't rent to you.

A. Why not?

B. We don't allow pets here. I'm sorry.

PRACTICE

That dog is yours.
        mine.
        his.
        hers.
        ours.
        theirs.

We don't allow pets here.
No pets allowed.
We don't allow dogs here.
No dogs allowed.
We don't allow children here.
No children allowed.

We don't allow pets here.
        dogs
        children

Trash Day

A. Oh, no! It's 6:45. We forgot to put out the trash.

B. What day is it?

A. Friday. It's trash day.

B. Let's hurry. Maybe we still have time.

PRACTICE

We forgot to put out the trash.
        lock the door.
        turn off the water.

Quiet!

A. Hey! Turn down that music. I'm trying to sleep.

B. What time is it?

A. It's 11:30. You have to be quiet after 10 P.M.

B. All right! All right!

PRACTICE

Turn down the music.	It's too loud.	I'm trying to sleep.
up TV.	soft.	rest.
off stereo.		relax.
on radio.		read.

apartment rules

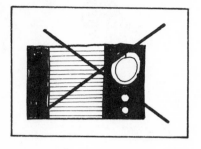 PUT OUT TRASH BY 7 A.M.

 NO CHILDREN

 NO VISITORS OVER 1 WEEK

 NO PETS

 NO NOISE AFTER 10

An Old Couch

A. I'm tired of this old couch.

B. We can't afford a new one.

A. Maybe we can reupholster it.
   What do you think?

B. That's a good idea!
   Let's check out some prices.

PRACTICE

I'm tired of this old couch.
          armchair.
          kitchen set.
          refrigerator.

Maybe we can reupholster it.
             fix
             repair
             clean
             paint

Call A Plumber

A. My sink is stopped up.

B. Did you try drain cleaner?

A. I tried everything. Nothing works.

B. All right. I'll call a plumber.

PRACTICE

I'll call a plumber.
        carpenter.
        painter.
        repair person.
     an electrician.

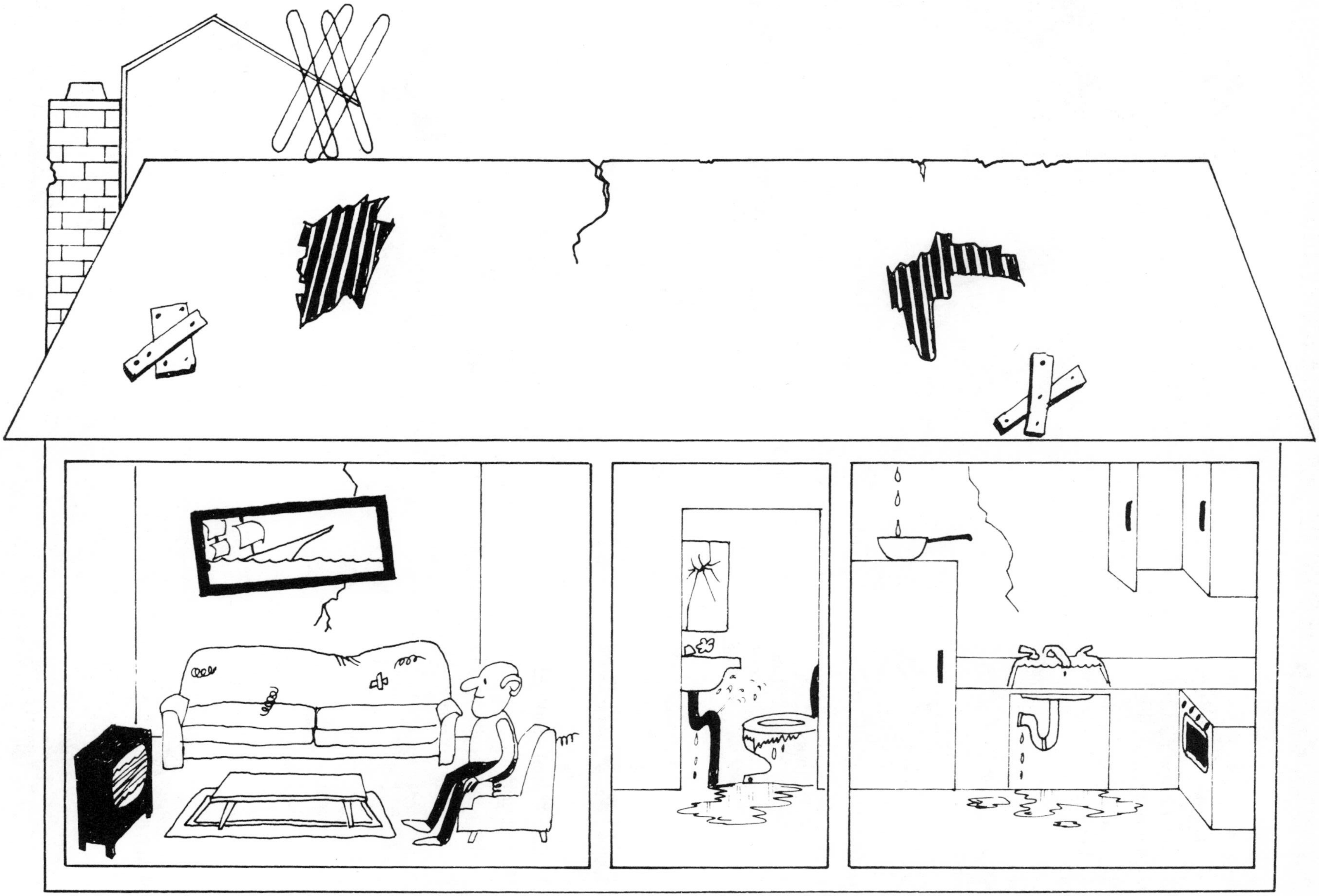

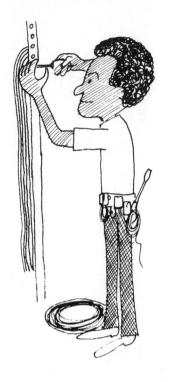

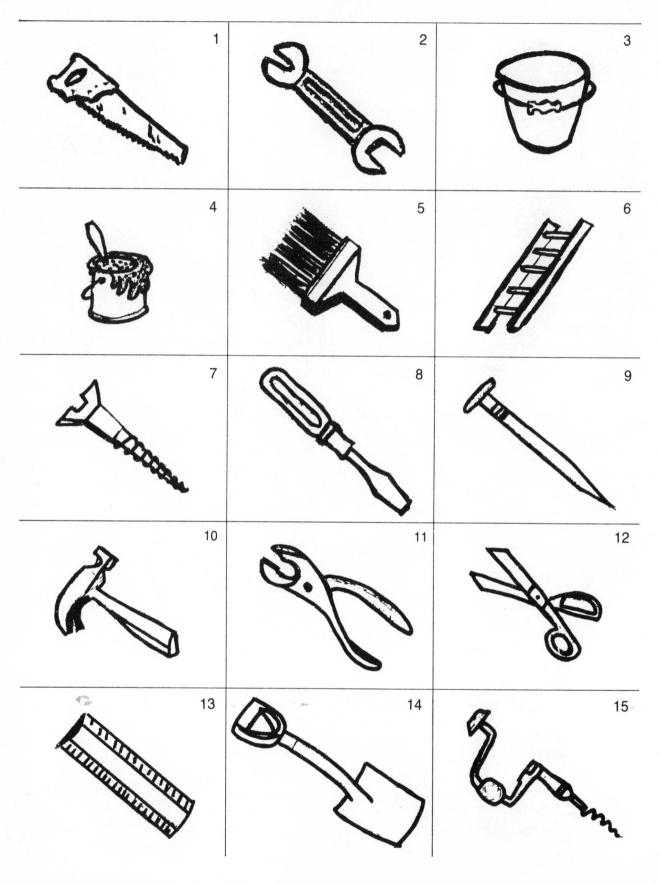

1

2

3

4

5

6

7

8

9

10

11

12

13

14

15

Choose A Color

A. We like the house, but the rooms need paint.

B. We plan to paint before you move in.

A. May I choose the colors?

B. Certainly. What colors would you like?

A. I think I'd like yellow in the kitchen and beige in the other rooms.

PRACTICE

We plan to paint.
        paper.
        repair.
        fix it up.
        clean it up.

I'd like beige.
        green.
        blue.
        red.
        yellow.
        brown.
        black.
        orange.
        purple.

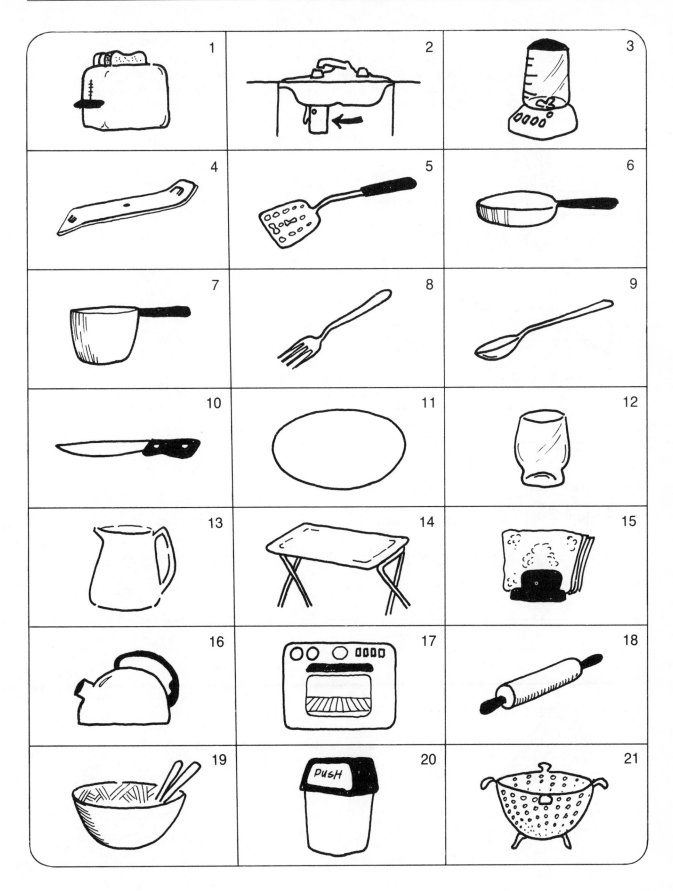

Mr. and Mrs Lee needed a one-bedroom apartment. They looked for one last week. They didn't find one, but they did find a studio apartment. It has one large room with a kitchen/dining room area, a bathroom, and a couch that opens to make a bed. The rent is $150 a month including utilities. The landlord wants a $50 cleaning deposit. The Lees will get the deposit back if the apartment is clean when they move out.

Questions

1. What kind of apartment did Mr. and Mrs. Lee need?
2. When did they look for an apartment?
3. What did they find?
4. What is a studio apartment?

Write the Word

1. Mr. and Mrs. Lee needed a one-bedroom _____.

2. They rented a _____apartment.

3. The rent is $150 a month including _____.

4. The landlord wanted a $50 cleaning _____.

Write About You

1. Do you live in an apartment or a house? _____

   _____

2. Do you rent the apartment (house)? _____

   _____

3. Did the landlord want a cleaning deposit? _____

   _____

4. Will you get the deposit back? _____

   _____

5. What rooms does your apartment or house have? _____

   _____

Using the Visuals

A. HOUSING ADS

Read each ad from the Housing Ads visual with the students. Put abbreviations on the board. Explain each abbreviation. Have the students role-play calling a landlord about one of the ads.

B. PLACES TO LIVE

1. Ask the students to identify each type of housing, and then tell which type they live in.

2. Discuss which types of housing are most common in the area of the country the class is located.

3. Ask where one would find many mobile homes, single houses, etc.

C. INSIDE THE HOUSE

1. Ask the students to name the rooms and the furnishings. Then have the students describe a room in their house.

2. Practice prepositions by asking the location of furniture. Elicit such responses as *upstairs, downstairs, between, in front of, behind, near, on.*

D. APARTMENT RULES

Looking at the Apartment Rules visual, have the students match each picture with the appropriate rule. Ask if their housing area has similar rules and regulations.

E. HOUSING REPAIRS

1. Looking at the Housing Repairs visual, have the students describe the problem:

   a. The roof is leaking.
   b. The antenna is bent.
   c. The wall is cracked.
   d. The sofa is broken.
   e. The TV is broken.
   f. The mirror is cracked.
   g. The pipe is broken.
   h. The toilet is overflowing.
   i. The sink is stopped up.

F. FIXING UP THE HOUSE AND YARD

1. Looking at the Fixing Up the House and Yard visual have the students name each person:

   a. Electrician
   b. Carpenter
   c. TV repair person
   d. Plumber
   e. Painter
   f. Gardener

2. Have the students tell which they would call to repair the house. (*Example:* I'd call the plumber to fix the toilet and sink. I'd call the carpenter (roofer) to fix the roof. I'd call the painter to paint the house.)

G. TOOLS

Using the Tools visual, have the students identify each tool (saw, wrench, pail, paint bucket, paintbrush, ladder, screw, screwdriver, nail, hammer, pliers, scissors, ruler, shovel, drill), and then have them tell what each is used for and which ones go together.

H. WORKING IN THE HOUSE

Looking at the Working in the House visual, have the students name each household item, then tell what each is used for. (*Example:* I use a vacuum cleaner to vacuum the floor. I use a mop to wash the floor. I use a broom to sweep the floor.)

I. IN THE KITCHEN

Using the In the Kitchen visual, have the students name the items. Then ask them if they have any of these. How often do they use each (every day, once in a while)?

Key:

toaster	glass
garbage disposal	pitcher
blender (food processor)	TV (snack) tray
bottle/can opener	napkins/napkin holder
pancake turner	teakettle
frying pan (skillet)	oven
saucepan	rolling pin
fork	salad bowl
spoon	trash can/wastebasket
knife	colander
placemat	

Supplemental Activities

A. LOCATING HOUSING AND   B. IDENTIFYING ROOMS AND FURNISHINGS

1. Have several pages of housing ads from the newspaper available. Ask the students to find an ad and read it to the class, explaining any abbreviations.

2. Ask the students to write an ad describing either their present housing or their "dream" house or apartment.

C. APARTMENT REGULATIONS

Have students tell about their own apartment and other rental regulations. Discuss similarities and differences.

D. MAINTENANCE PROBLEMS

1. Using the Tools, In the Kitchen, or Working in the House visuals as a guide, make picture bingo games, or write the vocabulary on the board and have students make their own bingo card. Play "Bingo."

2. Again using one of the three "item" visuals, pair the students. Have them ask and answer such questions as: Do you have a saw? A screwdriver? Do you vacuum your rugs? Sweep the floor? Have a toaster? Have a garbage disposal?

Clothing and Fabrics

COMPETENCY OBJECTIVES

On completion of this unit the students will show orally, in writing, or through demonstration that they are able to use the language needed to function in the following situations.

A. CLOTHING

    1. Identify most common articles of clothing.

    2. Describe clothing in terms of color, size, price.

    3. Explain clothing shopping needs.

    4. Exchange a clothing item.

B. FABRICS

    1. Identify most common fabrics.

    2. Identify most common sewing equipment.

    3. Explain information on clothing labels.

C. PURCHASING PROCEDURES

    1. Use cash, checks.

    2. Provide proper identification.

Pre-Post Assessment

A. CLOTHING

Using the Clothing 1 and 2 visuals, have the students name the clothing articles. Then have them role-play the following situations:

   a. A customer goes to a department store and asks for a certain item of clothing, giving color, size, and price.
   b. A customer asks a clerk where a certain clothing department is located.
   c. A customer asks a clerk to exchange a clothing item.

B. FABRICS

   1. Bring samples of common fabrics to class and ask students to identify each.

   2. Ask the students to name each item in the Sewing visual.

   3. Have the students answer the questions on the washing-care instruction sheet.

C. PURCHASING PROCEDURES

Have students role-play purchasing a clothing item and paying by check. Customer must provide two identifications.

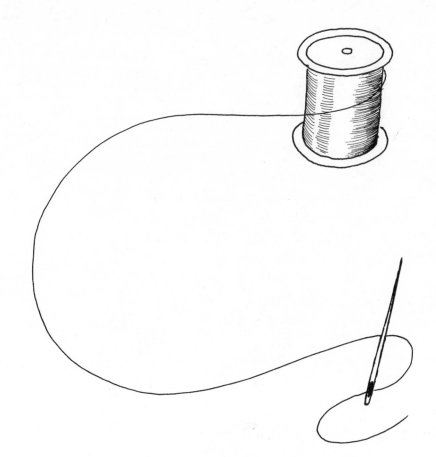

New Clothes For School

A. School is going to open in two weeks.
   The children need some new clothes.

B. What do they need?

A. Tommy needs shoes and pants.
   Helen needs a dress.

B. Why don't you take the kids shopping?
   They'll have to try on the clothes.

PRACTICE

I'm going to buy school clothes.
You're
He's/She's

I'm going to buy clothes.
           wear a shirt.
           look at shoes.
           try on

Tommy needs shoes.
           pants.
           jeans.
           socks.

We're going to buy school clothes.
You're
They're

Helen needs a dress.
                coat.
They need dresses.
               coats.

Tommy needs a pair of shoes.
                    pants.
                    jeans.
                    socks.

It's Too Tight

A. How does that fit?

B. I like the color,
   but it's too tight.

A. That was a size 8.
   Here's a size 10.
   I think it'll fit you better.

B. This is perfect.
   I'll wear it tomorrow.

PRACTICE

It's too tight.
   loose.
   long.
   short.
   small.

This is perfect.
   terrific.
   fine.
   great.

An Exchange

A. I bought this shirt for my father,
   but it's the wrong size.

B. Do you have your receipt?

A. Yes, here it is.

B. Do you want to exchange it,
   or do you want a refund?

A. I'd like to exchange it for a 15½–34.

PRACTICE

I bought a shirt yesterday.
   saw some coats
   went to the store
   read the ads
   wrote a check

I'd like to exchange it.
   return
   wear

A Good Buy

A. Look! Franklin's is having a sale.

B. Those pants were $25.00 last week.
They're on sale now and they're much cheaper.

A. Yes. They're $15.95.
That's a good buy.

PRACTICE

These pants are cheaper than those.
dresses	newer
shoes	larger
shirts	better

That's a good buy.   That's a good buy.
          deal.   better
          bargain.   the best

They're $15.95.
       $13.99.
       $69.00.
       $105.00.
       25¢.
       15¢.

Cash Or Charge?

A. How much is this sweater?

B. It's $8.99 plus tax.

A. Fine. I'll take it.

B. Cash or charge?

A. Cash.
   I don't have a charge account here.

PRACTICE

Cash or charge?
Cotton or wool?
Jacket or sweater?
Large or small?
Green or blue?
Yellow or white?

Cash.
I'll pay cash.
I'll charge it.
I'll write a check.
I'll use my credit card.

Two Identifications

A. That'll be $19.02.

B. I'm going to write a check.

A. I'll need to see two I.D.'s.

B. I have my driver's license and a credit card.

A. That's fine.

PRACTICE

I'm going to write a check.
          pay by

You need two I.D.'s.
                   identifications.

I have my driver's license and a credit card.
        student I.D.   check-cashing card.
        visa

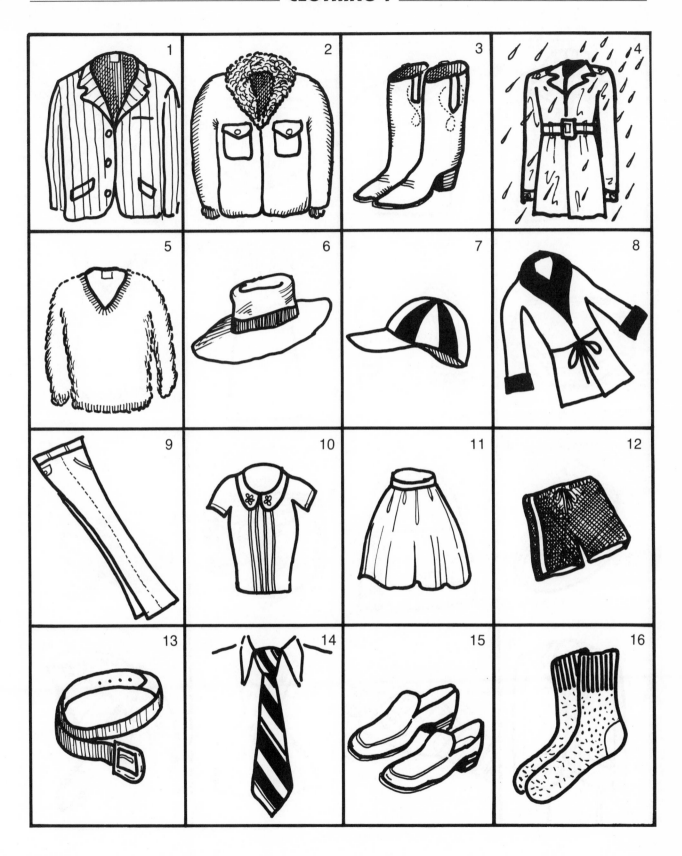

Buying Fabrics

A. Where's the yardage department?

B. It's on the second floor.
   What are you looking for?

A. I need a pattern and some material.
   I'm going to make a dress for myself.

B. What kind of material do you want?

A. I want a polyester and cotton blend.
   It doesn't need ironing.

PRACTICE

I'm going to make some clothes for myself.
You're   yourself.
He's   himself.
She's   herself.

We're going to make some clothes for ourselves.
You're   yourselves.
They're   themselves.

I need a pattern.
        a zipper.
        a pair of scissors.
        a spool of thread.
        buttons.

It doesn't need ironing.
                 pressing.
                 cleaning.

I want polyester.
        cotton.
        linen.
        wool.
        double-knit.

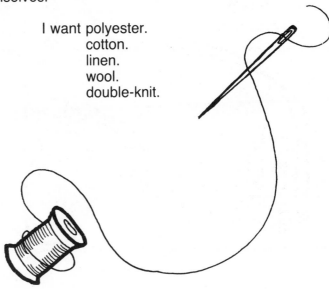

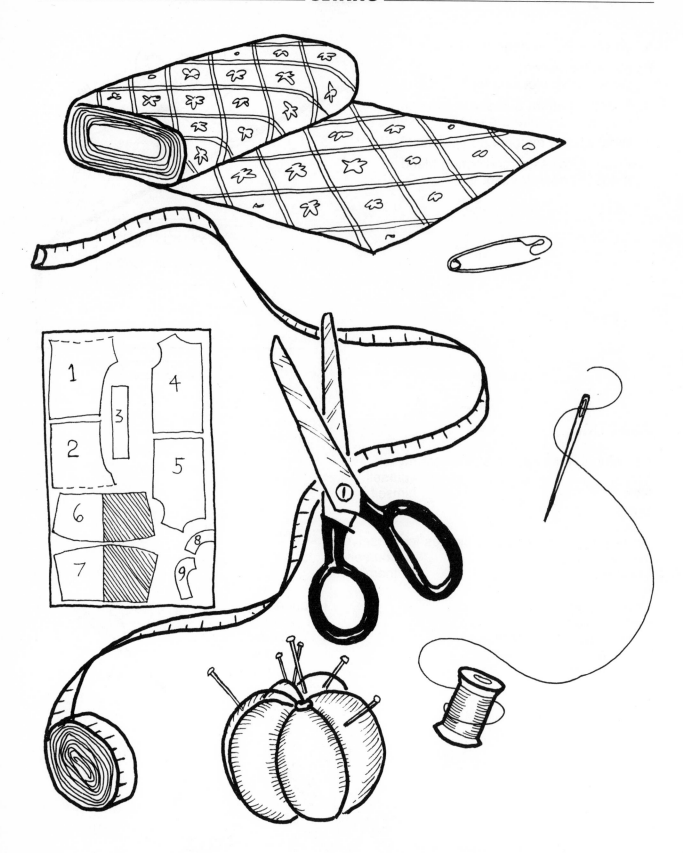

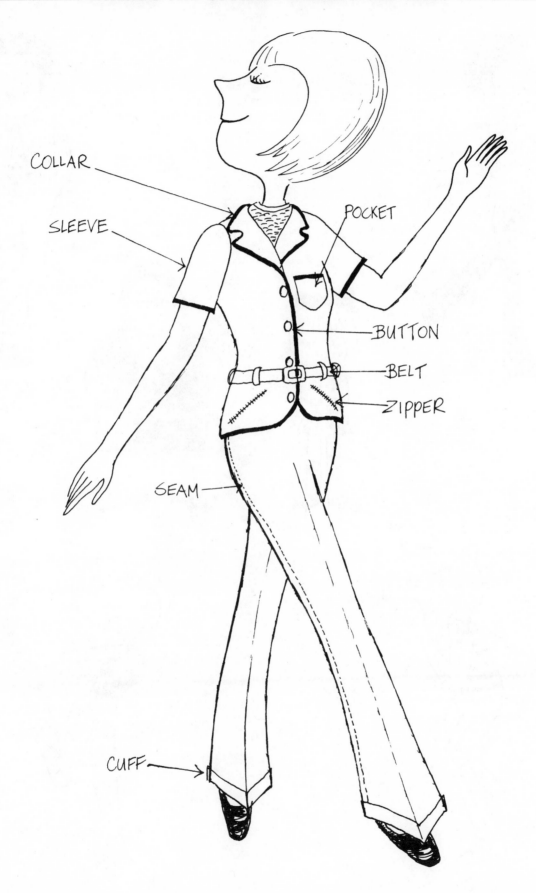

COLLAR

SLEEVE

POCKET

BUTTON

BELT

ZIPPER

SEAM

CUFF

Reading Labels

A. Mother! This sweater shrank.
   It's too small now.

B. You didn't wash it, did you?

A. Sure I did, why?

B. Look at the label. It says, DRY CLEAN ONLY.

PRACTICE

You didn't wash it, did you?
She   did she?
He   did he?

Look at the label.
          tag.
          instructions.

You didn't iron it, did you?
          bleach
          shrink

It says, DRY CLEAN ONLY.
          HAND WASH
          COOL WATER
          COOL IRON
          MACHINE WASH
          TUMBLE DRY

	Hand Wash Cold. Do Not Twist or Wring. Reshape. Dry Flat or Dry Clean.	sweater
	Machine Washable. Warm Water; Tumble Dry. Press on Wrong Side with Warm Iron.	shirt
	Hand Wash Separately. Line Dry. Warm Iron. Do Not Use Bleach.	skirt
	100% Cotton. Hand Woven. Made in India.	white shirt
	69% Cotton. 31% Polyester.	blue blouse

1. Can I hang the sweater up to dry?
   Can I put it in the washing machine?
   How can I dry it?

2. Can the shirt go into a machine dryer?
   Can you wash it with hot water?

3. How can I dry the skirt?
   Can I wash it with other clothes?

4. Will the white shirt shrink?
   Will the blue blouse shrink?

Mrs. Park always takes the children shopping before school opens. Tommy needs shoes and pants. Helen needs a dress. They try on their clothes in the store. They want their clothes to fit. Sometimes, when clothes don't fit, they have to return them. They get a refund or they exchange them. Mrs. Park also likes to buy clothes on sale. She saves money if she buys when everything is less expensive.

Questions

1. When does Mrs. Park take the children shopping?
2. What does Tommy need?
3. What does Helen need?
4. How do they know the clothes will fit?
5. Why does Mrs. Park like to buy clothes on sale?

Write the Word

1. Mrs. Park always goes _____ before school opens.

2. The children try _____ their clothes in the store.

3. They want their clothes to _____.

4. Sometimes, when clothes don't fit, they have to _____ them.

5. Mrs. Park likes to buy clothes on _____.

Write About You

1. Do you like to go shopping? _____

_____

2. What do you like to buy? _____

_____

3. Do you try on the clothes in the store? _____

_____

4. When do you exchange clothes? _____

_____

5. Why do you buy clothes on sale? _____

_____

READING EXERCISE—WASHING CLOTHES

We should be careful when we wash clothes. We should always read the label. If the label on a sweater says Dry Clean Only, we don't wash it. If we do, it will shrink. We only wash clothes in the washing machine when the label reads Machine Washable. Sometimes the label reads Hand Wash Separately. Then we should wash it in cool water by hand.

Questions

1. What should you read before you wash clothes?
2. What does Machine Washable mean?
3. What does Hand Wash Separately mean?
4. The label in a sweater reads Dry Clean Only. What will happen if you wash it in the machine?

Write the Word

1. We should always read the _____ on clothes.

2. We only wash clothes in the machine when the label reads

   _____.

3. Don't wash clothes in the machine when the label reads

   _____.

4. We should wash some clothes _____.

Write About You

1. Do you wash your own clothes? _____

   _____

2. Where do you wash clothes? _____

   _____

3. Do you read the labels in the clothes? _____

   _____

4. Tell how to wash the clothes you have on today. _____

   _____

Using the Visuals

A. CLOTHING 1 AND 2

   1. Ask the students to name the items:

      Key: Clothing 1

sport coat	jacket	boots	raincoat
sweater	hat	cap	robe
pants/slacks	blouse	shirt	shorts
belt	tie	shoes	socks

      Key: Clothing 2

shirt	T-shirt (undershirt)	briefs (undershorts)	pajamas
panties	bra	slip	nightgown
ring	purse	wallet	slippers
suit	watch	dress	umbrella

   2. Ask the students questions such as, "Do you have a . . . ," "Do you need a . . . ," "Do you want a . . . ?"

B. SEWING

Have the students identify the sewing notions:

Key (clockwise): material (fabric), safety pin, needle/thread, pincushion/straight pin, measuring tape, scissors, pattern.

C. WHERE'S THE COLLAR? WHERE'S THE CUFF?

Have the students identify parts of a suit as labeled. Identify similar parts on fellow students' clothing.

D. PRINT OR SOLID?

   1. Have students identify type of fabric design:

      Key (clockwise): checkered pants, polka-dot dress, print blouse/plaid pants, solid-color dress, pin-striped shirt/polka dot tie, striped shirt.

   2. Have the students identify similar fabric designs on fellow students' clothing.

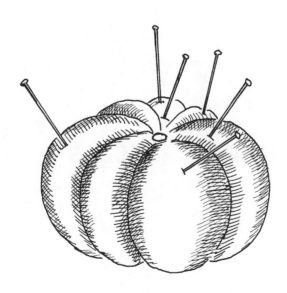

Supplemental Activities

A. CLOTHING

1. Have each student describe what another student is wearing. The other students must guess who it is.

2. Role-play buying an article of clothing. (Vocabulary to be used may be put on board at first—e.g., try on, size, dressing room, fit, how much).

3. Role play exchanging an article of clothing. Vocabulary—wrong size, wrong color, department manager, receipt, customer service.

4. Bring a laundry basket of clothing items to class. First, have students identify the articles, then have them give the color and guess the size. Ask students to try on certain articles of clothing that are obviously the wrong size. They should respond with such sentences as:

It's too long.	It's too short.
It's too big.	It's too small.
It's too tight.	It's too loose.
It fits.	It doesn't fit.

B. FABRICS

1. Bring samples of common fabrics to class. Ask students to identify each. Discuss washing/cleaning care for each.

2. Have students identify fabric used in clothing they are wearing.

7

Looking for a Job

COMPETENCY OBJECTIVES

On completion of this unit the students will show orally, in writing, or through demonstration that they are able to use the language needed to function in the following situations.

A. LOOKING FOR A JOB

   1. Read want ads relating to employment.

   2. Contact potential employers or agencies.

   3. Explain the purpose of a skills center.

B. MAKING AN APPOINTMENT; PREPARING FOR AN INTERVIEW

   1. Telephone to set up employment interview.

   2. Explain how to prepare for interview.

C. INTERVIEWING FOR A JOB

   1. Present a "positive image" (dress, posture, body language, general attitude).

   2. Ask questions concerning duties, hours, salary, qualifications, fringe benefits.

   3. Answer questions concerning personal background, education, experience.

D. FILING AN APPLICATION

   1. Complete the job application form.

   2. Make follow-up call.

Pre-Post Assessment

A. LOOKING FOR A JOB

  1. Using the Job Ads visual, have the students read the ads and explain the job information.

  2. Have the students role-play the following situations:

    a. Telephone in response to one of the newspaper ads and inquire about employment.

    b. Two students meet and talk about vocational training at the skills center.

B. MAKING AN APPOINTMENT FOR AN INTERVIEW

  1. Have students role-play telephoning to arrange an interview.

  2. Have students read and discuss the Employment Preparation information sheet.

C. INTERVIEWING FOR A JOB

  1. Using the Interview visual, have the students describe themselves as the prospective employees—how they are dressed, how they might conduct themselves, etc.

  2. Have the students role-play a job interview.

    a. The employee asks questions about duties, hours, salary, qualifications, fringe benefits.

    b. Employer asks and employee responds to questions concerning personal background, education, experience.

D. FILING AN APPLICATION

  1. Have the students fill out the job application form.

  2. Have the students role-play a follow-up call.

The Want Ads

A. I'm looking for a job.

B. What kind of work are you looking for?

A. In my country I was a mechanic.
I want to do the same thing here.

B. Why don't you look in the newspaper?

A. That's a good idea.

PRACTICE

What kind of work are you looking for?
                job
                tools
                car

Why don't you look in the newspaper?
                ask your friends?
                go to the employment office?
                check the bulletin board at the supermarket?

I   was a mechanic.
He/She   waiter.
                carpenter.
                fisherman.
                welder.
                cook.

Were you a secretary?
                student?
                teacher?
                nurse?

Reading The Want Ads

A. This ad for a mechanic sounds good.

B. What does it say?

A. It says "5-day week, salary plus commission, paid vacation, benefits."

B. Hey, that's good!
You should call right now.

PRACTICE

This ad sounds good.
     looks
     seems

It says "5-day week."
     $3.50 an hour.
     insurance.
     pension plan.
     benefits.

A Part-Time Job

A. Look! Did you see that one?

B. Uh huh. "Part-time gardener, after school and on weekends. Call Town House Apartments, 563-7851."

A. That's near where you live. Why don't you call?

B. I will. I need to earn some spending money.

PRACTICE

After school and on weekends.
Before   Sundays.

I need to earn some spending money.
      make   extra

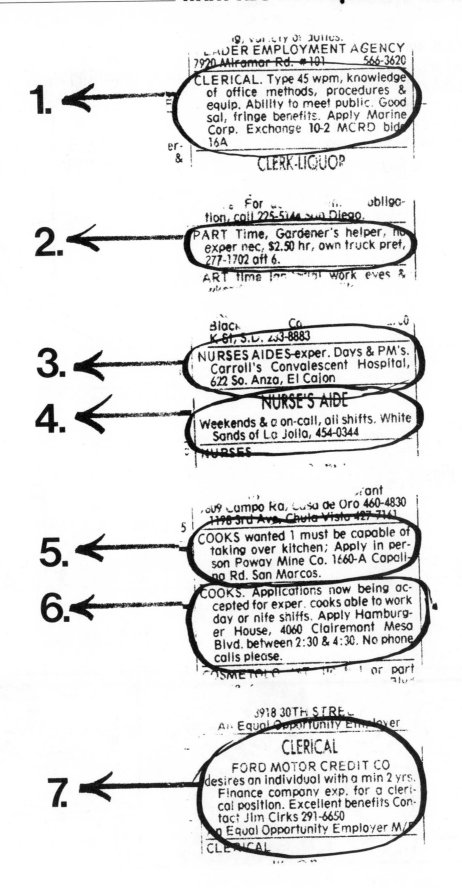

1. ...ADER EMPLOYMENT AGENCY
7920 Miramar Rd. #101 — 566-3620

CLERICAL. Type 45 wpm, knowledge of office methods, procedures & equip. Ability to meet public. Good sal, fringe benefits. Apply Marine Corp. Exchange 10-2 MCRD bldg 16A

CLERK-LIQUOR

2. ...For ... obligation, call 225-5144 San Diego.

PART Time, Gardener's helper, ho exper nec, $2.50 hr, own truck pref, 277-1702 aft 6.

ART time ... work eves &

3. Black Co. ...
K St, S.D. 233-8883

NURSES AIDES-exper. Days & PM's. Carroll's Convalescent Hospital, 622 So. Anza, El Cajon

4. NURSE'S AIDE

Weekends & a on-call, all shifts. White Sands of La Jolla, 454-0344

NURSES

5. ...ant
...609 Campo Rd, Casa de Oro 460-4830
1198 3rd Ave, Chula Vista 427-7141

COOKS wanted 1 must be capable of taking over kitchen; Apply in person Poway Mine Co. 1660-A Capalina Rd. San Marcos.

6. COOKS. Applications now being accepted for exper. cooks able to work day or nite shifts. Apply Hamburger House, 4060 Clairemont Mesa Blvd. between 2:30 & 4:30. No phone calls please.

COSMETOLO... or part

7. 3918 30TH STREE...
An Equal Opportunity Employer

CLERICAL

FORD MOTOR CREDIT CO desires an individual with a min 2 yrs. Finance company exp. for a clerical position. Excellent benefits Contact Jim Cirks 291-6650
An Equal Opportunity Employer M/...

CLERICAL

Vocational Training

A. I need a job, but I don't have any training.

B. Why don't you go to the skills center?
   You can get vocational training there.

A. What kind of training?

B. Auto body, mechanic, small appliance repair,
   upholstery, dry cleaning, welding . . .

A. Stop! I'm on my way.

PRACTICE

I don't have any training.
            experience.
            skills.

Why don't you go to the skills center?
                      vocational school?
                      trade school?

I'm Looking For A Job

A. Hello, Walker Employment Service.
B. I'm looking for a job. Can you help me?
A. Yes. Come in between 8 and 5.
   Go to the receptionist and she'll help you.

PRACTICE

Can you help me?
     answer my questions?
     type?
     take shorthand?

May I help you?
     have an application?
     see the manager?

A Good Impression

A. Wow! Why are you wearing that nice dress?
B. I'm going to a job interview.
   I want to make a good impression.
A. You look very businesslike.
   I'm sure they'll hire you.
B. I hope so. I'm willing to work very hard.

PRACTICE

I'm willing to work.
     learn.
     help.
     come early.
     stay late.

I'm willing to work hard.
I will work hard.
I intend to work hard.

Making An Appointment

A. Good afternoon. Personnel department.

B. This is Miss Nakamura. I'd like to make an appointment for an interview.

A. Have you sent in your application?

B. Yes, and I received a letter.
It said to call for an appointment.

A. Fine. Can you be here tomorrow at 3 P.M.?

B. Yes. I'll be there. Thank you.

PRACTICE

I have sent an application.
You have sent
He/She has sent

I have sent an application.
You have sent
He/She has sent

We have sent
You
They

You have sent an application.
He/She has

We have sent an application.
You have
They have

Have you sent in your application?
       telephoned?
       found a job?

Have not—haven't
Has not—hasn't

We have sent an application.
You have sent
They have sent

I have not sent an application.
You have not sent
He/She has not sent

We have not sent
You
They

Have you sent an application?
Has he/she sent

Have we sent an application?
Have you
Have they

A Job Interview

A. Miss Nakamura, I see from your application that you worked as a waitress. Are you looking for a full-time or part-time position?

B. I'm looking for a full-time job, but I would work part-time. What is the pay?

A. $2.90 an hour, plus tips. The job is on the late shift from 4 P.M. to 12 midnight, five days a week, Monday through Friday.

B. That's fine with me. I'm used to the late shift.

A. I have three more interviews. I'll let you know next week.

PRACTICE

I can work full-time.
              part-time.
              the night shift.

+ Plus tips
− Minus
× Times
÷ Divided by

I'm used to the night shift.
              day

I'm used to secretarial work.
You're   restaurant
He's/she's factory

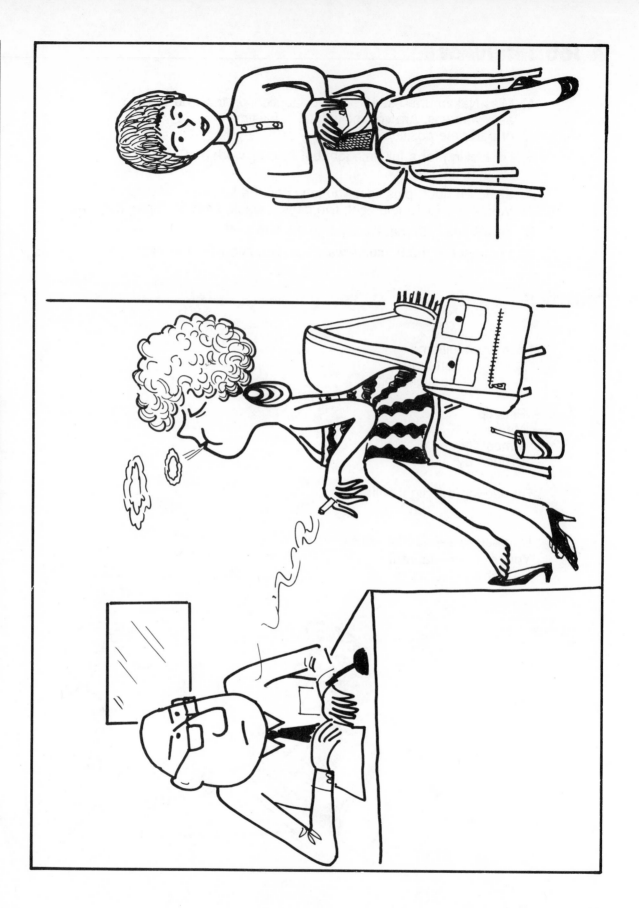

A Follow-Up Call

A. Hello. This is Susie Nakamura. I'm calling about the job
   I applied for last week. Is it still open?

B. I'm glad you called, Miss Nakamura. The job is yours.
   We planned to call you today. Can you start Monday?

A. Yes! I'll be there. Should I come in a little early?

B. That's a good idea. We'll give you a uniform
   and show you around.

PRACTICE

I will be there
You
He/she

We will be there
You
They

I will be there
You
He/she

I will not be there
You
He/she

You will be there
They

Will you be there?
Will they

Is it still open?
       closed?
       available?

JUNE

S	M	T	W	T	F	S
. .	. .	. .	. .	1	2	3
4	(5)	6	7	8	9	10
11	12	13	14	15	16	17
18	19	20	21	22	23	24
25	26	27	28	29	30	. .

My First Paycheck!

A. I got my first paycheck today!

B. How much did you make?

A. I made $184, but I only got $139.60.

B. That's because they take out federal and state taxes, and Social Security.

A. Wow! So many deductions!

PRACTICE

How much did you make?
              earn?
              receive?

They take out taxes.
          deduct
          withhold

GREEN TOOL COMPANY

"Tools for you since 1922"

Statement of earnings
and payroll deductions

Employee No. _763_   Date _July 1, 1975_

Total Hours	Rate	Regular Earnings	Overtime Earnings	Gross Earnings	Federal Tax	State Tax	FICA	Total Deduc.
40	4.60 hr	184.00	- -	184.00	20.40	6.00	18.00	44.40

Period Ending _6-3-75_   NET PAY ___ $139.60

APPLICATION FOR EMPLOYMENT

1. Title of position _____ Beginning date _____

2. Name   Mr.
        Mrs. _____
        Miss   Last (Print)   First   Middle   (Maiden Name)

3. Address _____ Home Telephone _____
       Street and Number   City   State   Zip Code

4. Age _____ Date of birth _____ Social Security No. _____ / ___ / _____ U.S. Citizen ____

5. Marital Status: Single _____   Married _____   Widowed _____   Divorced _____

6. In case of accident, notify _____ Address _____ Phone _____

7. Circle the highest grade you completed in each school	Name and location of school	Dates
High School 9 10 11 12		
College 1 2 3 4		
Col. Post-grad: Sem. Hrs.___		
Professional or Voc. Schools		

8. List your jobs for the last five years.

From Mo./Yr.	To Mo./Yr.	Employer's Name, Address, Telephone Number, and Name of Last Supervisor	Salary	Position	Reason for Leaving

9. What are your hobbies and interests? _____

_____

10. _____ Date _____
          Signature

A. LOOKING FOR A JOB

   1. Look in the want ads in the newspaper to find out about available jobs.

   2. Go to a public or private employment agency that finds work for people. Public agencies are fine. Private agencies charge a fee if they find a job for a person.

   3. Go to a prospective employer—a company, corporation, agency, or other organization—to inquire about available jobs.

B. APPLYING FOR A JOB

   1. Go to the employer and inquire directly.

   2. Mail a job application.

C. PREPARING FOR A JOB INTERVIEW

   1. Be prepared to give your address, telephone number, and Social Security number.

   2. Have ready your driver's license and other identification cards. You may be asked for a health certificate.

   3. Be able to give your work record: name and locations of previous employers, dates of your employment, wages, and description of your work. You will probably be asked the reasons for leaving.

   4. Dress neatly and appropriately.

   5. Go to the interview alone. Do not bring friends or relatives to the interview. It is a good idea to carry a list of the necessary information with you.

D. DURING THE INTERVIEW

   1. Tell your qualifications for the job and your interest in it.

   2. Be businesslike and brief.

   3. Be realistic in discussing wages.

   4. Do not talk about personal or money problems. Discuss matters related to the job.

   5. Do not worry if you don't get the first job you apply for. There will be other opportunities.

READING EXERCISE—LOOKING FOR A JOB

Miss Nakamura is looking for a job. In her country she was a waitress. Every day she looked in the newspaper. Last week she went to an employment service and they helped her. They sent her for an interview. First, she called the personnel department and made an appointment. She also sent in an application. She looked very nice on the day of the interview. She wanted to make a good impression. The interviewer asked her many questions. He asked if Miss Nakamura wanted to work full-time or part-time. She said she would like to work full-time. Now she has a job. She makes $2.90 an hour plus tips. She works from 4 P.M. to 12 midnight. She is very happy.

Questions

1. What kind of work was Miss Nakamura looking for?
2. Where did she go last week to get help?
3. What did she send in before the interview?
4. Why did she want to look nice?
5. Did she want to work full-time or part-time?
6. How much money does she make?

Write the Word

1. Miss Nakamura is looking for a _____.

2. In her country she worked as a _____.

3. Last week she went to an _____.

4. They sent her for an _____.

5. First she called the personnel department and made an _____.

6. She looked nice for the interview. She wanted to make a good

   _____.

Write About You

1. Do you work? _____

   _____

2. What is your occupation? _____

   _____

3. Did you work in your country? _____

   _____

4. What kind of work did you do? _____

   _____

5. What kind of job would you like to have? _____

   _____

Using the Visuals

A. JOB ADS

Have the students read the ads. Write abbreviations and complete words on board.

wpm = words per minute
exper = experience
nec = necessary
pref = preferred
min = minimum

B. OCCUPATIONS 1 AND 2

Ask the students to identify the occupations.

Key:

policeman	secretary
firefighter	cook
fisherman	seamstress
mail carrier	mechanic
doctor/nurse	welder
housewife	dentist

C. THE INTERVIEW

Have the students describe how each job applicant is dressed. Discuss how the interviewer might feel. Make a list of opposites. (Example: casual—businesslike, prepared—unprepared, smoker—nonsmoker, employed—unemployed.)

Supplemental Activities

A. LOOKING FOR A JOB

1. Have several job ads sections available from the newspaper. Ask each student to find a job that interests him or her.

2. Pair the students and have them role-play telephoning in response to the ad, going for an interview, making a follow-up call.

B. MAKING AN APPOINTMENT; PREPARING FOR AN INTERVIEW

1. Discuss the Employment Preparation sheet with students. Stress the do's and don'ts.

C. INTERVIEWING FOR A JOB

1. Have the students make up an imaginary person, listing all that person's personal data and qualifications. Let different students pretend to be this person during a job interview. (Students may want to make up a poor candidate for contrast.) The applicant may act sloppy, lazy, disinterested.

2. Have students read, interpret and discuss payroll deductions as shown on page 134.

D. FILING AN APPLICATION

1. Have each student prepare the Application for Employment form and save a copy for reference.

Banking and Postal Services

COMPETENCY OBJECTIVES

On completion of this unit the students will show orally, in writing or through demonstration that they are able to use the language needed to function in the following situations.

A. BANKING

    1. Differentiate between checking and savings accounts.

    2. Make a deposit or withdrawal.

    3. Fill out and cash a personal check.

B. POST OFFICE

    1. Buy stamps.

    2. Mail package or letter.

    3. Buy a postal money order.

    4. Register or insure mail.

Pre-Post Assessment

A. BANKING

   1. Have the students role-play the following situations:

      a. Inquiring about opening a checking and savings account.
      b. Making a deposit or withdrawal from the new account.
      c. Endorsing and cashing a personal check.

B. POST OFFICE

   1. Using the Post Office visual, have the students explain the services that are obtained at the post office.

      a. Buying stamps.
      b. Mailing a package.
      c. Buying a postal money order.
      d. Registering or insuring mail.

Checking Or Savings?

A. I'd like to open an account, please.

B. Checking or savings?

A. What's the difference?

B. In a checking account you deposit money and write checks to pay bills.

A. I see . . . and what's a savings account?

B. You deposit money and leave it there to earn interest. You withdraw it only for an emergency.

PRACTICE

You deposit money.
    put in
    withdraw
    take out

Put the cash in.
    money
    deposit
    check

Take the cash out.
    money
    deposit
    check

You withdraw money for an emergency.
                    special purchases.

Put in the cash.
    money.
    deposit.
    check.

Take out the cash.
    money.
    deposit.
    check.

Opening A Checking Account

A. I'd like to open a checking account, please.

B. The minimum deposit is $100. How much would you like to deposit today?

A. $150.00

B. Fill out this form and I'll give you some temporary checks. You'll receive your personalized checks in the mail.

A. Thank you.

PRACTICE

The minimum is $100.00.
   maximum

You'll receive your personalized checks.
                              stationery.
                              license plates.

FOR DEPOSIT TO THE ACCOUNT OF

JOHN R. SMITH
ROSE A. SMITH
736 Pine St. 492-7770
San Diego, Calif. 92110

DATE_____ 19_____

_____
SIGN HERE FOR LESS CASH IN TELLERS PRESENCE

FIRST WORLD BANK
2200 Main Street
San Diego, Calif. 92111

CASH	CURRENCY		
	COIN		
LIST CHECKS SINGLY			
TOTAL FROM OTHER SIDE			
TOTAL			
LESS CASH RECEIVED			
NET DEPOSIT			

5471

90-1522
1222

USE OTHER SIDE FOR
ADDITIONAL LISTING

BE SURE EACH ITEM IS
PROPERLY ENDORSED

⑆122215223⑆011302444⑈ 5471

FIRST BANK

NEXT TELLER

NEW ACCOUNTS

WAIT HERE

LOANS

JOHN R. SMITH
ROSE A. SMITH
736 Pine St.   492-7770
San Diego, Calif.   92110

206

_____ 19____   90-59 / 1222

PAY TO THE
ORDER OF _____ $ _____

_____ DOLLARS

FIRST WORLD BANK
2200 Main Street
San Diego, Calif.   92111

MEMO _____   _____

⑃:1222⑃0059⑃:0041311531⑃ 0 206

JOHN R. SMITH
ROSE A. SMITH
736 Pine St.   492-7770
San Diego, Calif.   92110

206

_____ 19____   90-59 / 1222

PAY TO THE
ORDER OF _____ $ _____

_____ DOLLARS

FIRST WORLD BANK
2200 Main Street
San Diego, Calif.   92111

MEMO _____   _____

⑃:1222⑃0059⑃:0041311531⑃ 0 206

JOHN R. SMITH
ROSE A. SMITH
736 Pine St.   492-7770
San Diego, Calif.   92110

206

_____ 19____   90-59 / 1222

PAY TO THE
ORDER OF _____ $ _____

_____ DOLLARS

FIRST WORLD BANK
2200 Main Street
San Diego, Calif.   92111

MEMO _____   _____

⑃:1222⑃0059⑃:0041311531⑃ 0 206

Buying A Money Order

A. I want to buy a money order for $25.00.

B. Here you are. That's $25.80. You fill in "pay to" and "purchased by." You keep the top copy and send the bottom copy.

A. Thank you.

Customer's Receipt

U.S. Postal Service	Pay to: Gas & Electric
	          5671 Twelfth Ave.
	Purchased by:
	  Sarah Black
	  220 Main St.
		Not Negotiable

Cashing A Money Order

A. I want to cash this money order.

B. Is it made out to you?

A. Yes. It's from my mother in Canada.

B. Do you have any identification?

A. Will my driver's license do?

B. That's fine. Endorse it on the back. Sign your name exactly as it is on the front.

PRACTICE

Will my driver's license do?
    passport   be satisfactory?
    student visa
    credit card

Endorse it on the back.
Sign
Put your signature

Let's Go To The Post Office

A. Have you mailed the bills yet?
It's already the 10th of the month.

B. No, I haven't. I'm out of stamps.

A. Well, let's go to the post office and get some.

B. O.K. If the windows are closed we can use the machines in the lobby.

PRACTICE

Have you mailed it yet?
    sent
    stamped
    sealed

I haven't mailed it yet.
    seen
    bought
    read

I've already mailed it.
    seen
    bought
    read

Sending Important Mail

A. I want to make sure my son receives this letter.
   It has his high school diploma in it.

B. You can send it either by certified mail or registered mail.

A. Which do you recommend?

B. If you *only* want to make sure it is received, send it by certified mail.
   It's less expensive.

A. O.K. How about this package?

B. What's in it?

A. A watch.

B. You should insure it for the value of the watch, and send it by
   registered mail. It's more expensive, but it's the safest way.

PRACTICE

Either certified mail	*or*	registered mail.
postal money order		bank money order.
cash		check.
regular mail		special delivery.

It's less expensive.
   more difficult.

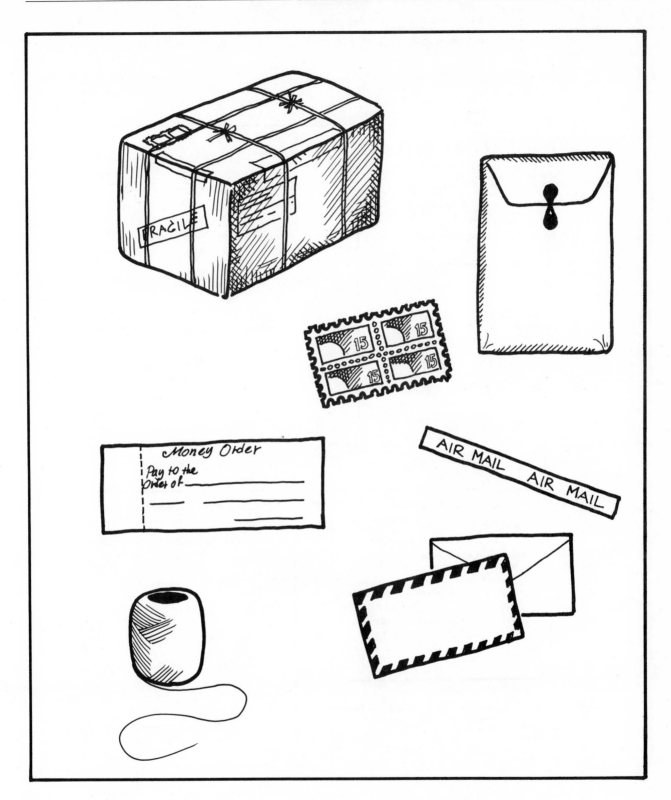

Pretend you are sending a package to your country—complete the following forms.

INSTRUCTIONS GIVEN BY SENDER
Dispositions de l'expéditeur

Sender must check alternative disposition desired.
IF UNDELIVERABLE AS ADDRESSED:
Au cas de non-livraison, le colis doit être:

☐ **Return to sender. Return charges guaranteed.**
Renvoyé à l'expéditeur, qui s'engage à payer les frais de retour.

☐ **Forward to:** *Réexpédié à M.:*

☐ **Abandon.** *Abandonné.*

(Sender—*Expéditeur*)

(Address of sender—*Adresse de l'expéditeur*)

(City, State—*Ville, Province, Département*)

To

(Name of addressee—*Nom du destinataire*)

(Street and number—*Rue et numéro*)

(City, Province, State, etc.—*Ville, Province, Département, etc.*)

(Country—*Pays*)

(*Sender must comply with U. S. export control regulations.*)
(*Complete both sides of tag*)

THIS LABEL FOR INTERNATIONAL PARCEL POST USE. COMPLETE AND APPLY ON ADDRESS SIDE OF PARCEL. BEND AT SLIT AND PEEL OFF BACKING.

PARCEL POST CUSTOMS DECLARATION — UNITED STATES OF AMERICA

INSTRUCTIONS GIVEN BY SENDER
Dispositions de l'Expéditeur

If undeliverable as addressed:
Au cas de non-livraison:

☐ Return to sender. Return charges guaranteed.
Le colis doit être renvoyé à l'expéditeur, qui s'engage à payer les frais de retour.

☐ Forward to. (*Le colis doit être réexpédié à*):

☐ Abandon. (*Abandon du colis.*)

(Sender's Signature—*Signature de l'expéditeur*)

QTY	USE INK OR TYPEWRITER ITEMIZED LIST OF CONTENTS	VALUE (U.S. $)

MAILING OFFICE DATE STAMP	LBS.
	OZS.
	POSTAGE $

ACCEPTING CLERK'S INITIALS	INSURED VALUE (U.S. $)

PS Form 2966-A, June 1972

Maria wants to open a checking account. With a checking account she can deposit money and write checks to pay bills. In her bank, the minimum deposit is $100.00. Maria will receive personalized checks to use. Today Maria received her paycheck from work. She earned $80.00 but only got $65.00. That's because she had a lot of federal and state deductions. She deposited her paycheck in her new checking account.

Questions

1. What kind of banking account did Maria want?
2. What is the minimum deposit?
3. Why did Maria receive only $65.00 in her paycheck?

Write the Word

1. Maria wants to open a _____.

2. Maria will receive _____ checks to use.

3. Maria has to pay a lot of federal and state _____.

Write About You

1. Do you have a checking account in a bank? _____

_____

2. Do you have a savings account? _____

_____

3. How can the bank help you? _____

_____

When Mrs. Park is out of stamps, she goes to the post office. If the windows are closed, she uses the machines in the lobby. Sometimes she has something important to mail. If she wants to make sure it is received, she sends it by certified mail. If it is something very expensive, she insures it. It costs a little more money, but it's the safest way.

Questions

1. Where does Mrs. Park go to buy stamps?
2. How does she send important mail?
3. How does she send something expensive?

Write the Word

1. When Mrs. Park is out of stamps, she goes to the _____.

2. If she has something important to send, she sends it by

   _____ mail.

3. If it is something expensive, she _____ it.

Write About You

1. Do you send letters? _____

   _____

2. Where do you buy stamps? _____

   _____

3. Have you sent a letter by certified mail? _____

   _____

4. Have you sent a letter by registered mail? _____

   _____

5. Have you insured mail? _____

   _____

6. What do you get at the post office? _____

   _____

Using the Visuals

A. THE BANK

   1. Have the students identify the major bank services:

      a. Checking and savings accounts
      b. Safety deposit boxes
      c. Statement window
      d. Loans

B. THE POST OFFICE

   1. Have the students describe the activities taking place in the post office:

      a. Buying a money order.
      b. Mailing a package.
      c. Mailing a letter.
      d. Checking his post office box.
      e. Addressing envelopes.

C. MAILING

   1. Have the students tell what they need:

      a. A money order
      b. Four stamps
      c. Air mail envelopes
      d. A mailing bag
      e. To wrap the package

Supplemental Activities

A. BANKING

   1. Have the students fill out sample deposit and withdrawal slips.

   2. Have the students practice writing sample checks to each other, for utility bills, to supermarkets.

B. POST OFFICE

   1. If possible have the students write a simple letter in English to a friend or relative. Discuss the proper procedure for addressing an envelope using the return address and complete address including zip codes.

   2. Have the students fill in the forms for mailing a package outside the country.

Community Resources

COMPETENCY OBJECTIVES

On completion of this unit the students will show orally, in writing, or through demonstration that they are able to use the language needed to function in the following situations.

A. PUBLIC LIBRARY

Identify and use local library services.

B. PUBLIC PARKS AND RECREATIONAL SERVICES

Identify and locate local facilities.

C. DAY CARE CENTERS

Locate and register children in day care centers.

D. PUBLIC SCHOOLS

Locate and register children in neighborhood schools.

E. PUBLIC HEALTH AGENCIES AND OTHER COMMUNITY RESOURCES

Locate and describe services of agencies.

Pre-Post Assessment

A. PUBLIC LIBRARY

Using the Library visual, have the students locate and identify the sections and services in a public library.

B. PUBLIC PARKS AND RECREATIONAL SERVICES

Using the Recreation visual, have the students name the various recreation areas and describe local facilities.

C. DAY CARE CENTERS

Have the students role-play enrolling a preschool child in a day care center.

D. PUBLIC SCHOOLS

Have the students role-play enrolling a child in elementary school, including verifying the child's age and presenting the immunization record.

E. PUBLIC HEALTH AGENCIES AND OTHER COMMUNITY RESOURCES

Using the In the Community visual, have the students locate the various community services; have them locate and tell about similar agencies in the local area.

A. I have to write a report for school, but I don't have the books I need.

B. Go to the library. You can get a library card today, and take the books home.

A. What do I need to get a card?

B. You need proof of where you live.

A. What kind of proof do I need?

B. You can show a bill, a letter addressed to you, or a driver's license.

PRACTICE

You need proof of where you live.
           verification
           evidence

You can get books at the library.
           talking books
           magazines
           reference materials
           records
           tapes
           pictures

A Day In The Park

A. It's a beautiful day!
Let's go to the park.

B. What can we do there?

A. We can go to the zoo, the museums,
or walk in the gardens.

B. That's a good idea.
Wait a minute, and I'll pack a lunch.

PRACTICE

We can go to the museums.
              Art Museum.
              Natural History Museum.
              Museum of Man.

We can go to the Space Theater.
              Puppet Theater.
              Performing Arts Theater.
              Organ Pavillion.

We can ride the train.
              merry-go-round.
              bus in the zoo.

We can look at the gardens.
              flowers.
              dancers.
              jugglers.

We can listen to the concert.
              musicians.
              band.

In The Snow

A. We went to the mountains last week.

B. Was there a lot of snow?

A. Plenty! The kids went ice-skating and tried new sleds. We built a snowman, too.

B. I'm sure you had fun.

PRACTICE

Was there a lot of snow?
              sleet?
              rain?
              fog?

The kids tried out their new sleds.
                                      skates.
                                      skis.

Sightseeing

A. John and Sally will arrive next week.
Where are we going to take them?

B. We took them to the zoo last time.
How about the lighthouse this time?

A. Yes, and let's stop later for dinner at the Old Inn.

B. I think they'll enjoy that.

PRACTICE

We took them to the zoo.
       lighthouse.
       park.
       museum.
       lake.
       mountains.

Where are we going to take them?
    will we   eat?
          visit?
          go?

Camping

A. What did you do last weekend?

B. We went camping at Highlands State Park.

A. Did you sleep outside?

B. Yes, the weather was beautiful. We went fishing on Saturday. I caught seven fish!

A. That's nice. But I'm not much for the outdoor life.

PRACTICE

We went camping.
     fishing.
     swimming.
     boating.
     sailing.
     hiking.
     skiing.

I'm not much for the outdoor life.
     concerts.
     shopping.
     reading.
     TV.

1.

2.

3.

4.

5.

6.

7.

8.

9.

Day Care Centers

    A. I must get a job.
          First I have to go back to school to learn more English.

    B. What are you going to do with the children?

    A. Well, Jose is in first grade now, and I'm going to put Carlos into a
          day care center.

    B. I've never thought of that. Is it expensive?

    A. No, we pay according to our income.

PRACTICE

I must   get a job.
I have to learn English.
         earn money.
         go back to school.
         find a day care center.

We pay according to our income.
                to our ability.
         only what we can afford.

Public Health Services

A. I have to register my son for kindergarten.

B. Do you have his birth certificate and immunization record?

A. I have the birth certificate, but his shots aren't up-to-date.

B. At the Public Health Department you can get free shots.
Be sure to call before you go. They'll tell you
the nearest location and the clinic day.

PRACTICE

I have to register my son for preschool.
                kindergarten.
                elementary school.
                junior high school.
                senior high school.

Do you have his immunization records?
                vaccination
                shot
                health

He needs a smallpox vaccination.
            polio immunization.
            rubella immunization.
            mumps immunization.
       DPT shots.

Legal Aid

A. We've just moved out of our apartment.
   They won't give us our deposit back.

B. Did you leave it clean?

A. Yes, we did. It was spotless.

B. Why don't you see a lawyer?

A. We don't know one.
   Lawyers are expensive, and we're broke.

B. Try the Legal Aid Society.
   Someone there can help you.

PRACTICE

We've just moved out of our apartment.
      recently

They won't give us our deposit back.
      help us.
      refund our money.

It was spotless.
He   careless.
She is penniless.

```
CHANGE OF ADDRESS CARD
_____
_____
_____
       NEW ADDRESS
_____
_____
_____
```

```
          MONEY ORDER
Pay to the
Order of  _____

          50.00
          _____

_____   _____
```

How Do I Get To . . . ?

A. How do I get to the Department of Motor Vehicles?
   I need to renew my license.

B. We're on Main Street now. Go up Main Street to Palm.
   Turn right and go to the middle of the block.
   It'll be on your right.

A. O.K. Thanks.

PRACTICE

How do I get to the D.M.V.?
    go   fire station?
    find   synagogue?
             welfare department?
             Social Security office?

Go up Main Street.
    down
    right on
    left on

1. LEGAL AID CLINIC
2. HOSPITAL
3. SOCIAL SECURITY OFFICE
4. WELFARE DEPARTMENT
5. PUBLIC LIBRARY
6. RECREATION CENTER

7. DEPARTMENT OF MOTOR VEHICLES
8. CHURCH
9. FIRE STATION
10. POLICE STATION
11. EMPLOYMENT OFFICE
12. SYNAGOGUE

When mothers go to work or school, they can take their children to day care centers. They pay according to their income. Of course, when children are older, they go to public school. Before you can register a child for kindergarten, you have to have his or her birth certificate and immunization record. You can go to a public health clinic for immunization shots and TB tests. They are free there. You can call the health department to find the clinic nearest you.

Questions

1. Where can mothers take small children when they work?
2. How do they pay?
3. What must you have before you register a child for kindergarten?
4. Where can you go for free immunization shots?

Write the Word

1. When mothers work, they can take their children to _____.

2. They pay according to their _____.

3. Before you register a child for kindergarten, you have to have his or her

   _____ and _____ record.

4. You can get free shots at the _____.

Write About You

1. Do you have small children? _____

   _____

2. Do they go to school? Where? _____

   _____

3. Is there a public health clinic near you? _____

   _____

There are many things to do in a big city. If you want to read, you can borrow books from the library. You can go to the park on beautiful days. In the park you can go to the zoo or to the museums. You can look at the gardens or ride the merry-go-round. If you like the water, you can swim or go for a boat ride. If there are mountains close to the city, you can go camping. When you go camping, you can sleep in a sleeping bag.

Questions

1. Where do you go to read or borrow books?
2. What can you do in the park?
3. Where can you go camping?

Write the Word

1. There are many things to do in _____.

2. You can borrow books from the _____.

3. In the park you can go to the _____ or to the

   _____.

4. If you like the water, you can _____ or go for a

   _____ ride.

5. You can go camping in the _____.

6. When you go camping, you sleep in a _____.

Write About You

1. Do you go to the library? _____

   _____

2. Do you have a library card? _____

   _____

3. What kind of books do you like? _____

   _____

4. Do you go to the park? _____

   _____

5. What do you like to do at the park? _____

_____

6. Do you like to swim or go for a boat ride? _____

_____

7. Have you been camping? Where? _____

_____

8. What do you like to do for recreation? _____

_____

Using the Visuals

A. THE LIBRARY

    1. Have the students describe these library facilities:

        a. Return book section
        b. Checkout section
        c. New books area
        d. Children's books
        e. Reference section
        f. Taped books
        g. Magazines
        h. Information

B. THE WEATHER

    1. Have the students describe the weather when it's:

        a. A nice day
        b. Smoggy
        c. Raining
        d. Cloudy
        e. Stormy

C. RECREATION

    1. Have the students name the recreation facilities or place of interest.

    Key:

zoo	lake/fishing	mountains/camping
beach	mission	recreation center
observatory	lighthouse	park/museum

D. IN THE COMMUNITY

    1. Have the students locate each community resource or agency on the Community visual. Then have them find a similar agency in their own city or neighborhood. If possible, make a local community map. Have the students look up the telephone numbers for each community agency in the local area.

    2. Ask the students where each community agency is located. Elicit responses such as,"It's on the corner of Palm and North Avenue." Pair the students. Have them ask directions of one another.

    3. Give a location and ask directions to another building. (Example: I'm at the Legal Aid Clinic. How do I get to the Department of Motor Vehicles?) Have students give directions using such terms as "two blocks north/south, turn right/left," etc. At first it may be necessary to practice direction vocabulary.

    4. Set up situations such as:

        a. If I need a driver's license, I go to the _____.
        b. If I need a job, I go to the _____.
        c. If I need an operation, I go to the _____.
        d. If I need a Social Security card, I go to the _____.

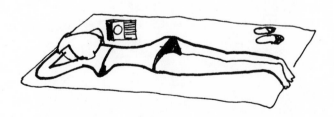

Supplemental Activities

A. THE LIBRARY

    1. If possible, visit the library nearest the school. When arrangements are made, the librarian may schedule a talk or film and give the students a tour.

    2. Have the students role-play applying for a library card and looking for books in the card catalog (author, subject, title cards).

B. PUBLIC PARKS AND RECREATION SERVICES

Have the students tell where they go on weekends or vacations. Do they have similar facilities in their native countries?

C. DAY CARE CENTERS

Have the students role-play enrolling a child in a day care center. If possible, have one student call a center in the local area to obtain pertinent information.

D. PUBLIC SCHOOLS

Have the students role-play enrolling a child in elementary school. (One student plays a secretary, one a parent; parent has age and immunization records.)

E. PUBLIC HEALTH AND COMMUNITY RESOURCES

Locate the public health office in the school area. Find out when the clinic day is and what shots are given. Have more able students call and report on the information.